THEY MET AT PHILIPPI

THEY MET AT PHILIPPI

A Devotional Commentary on Philippians

By the Reverend Carroll E. Simcox, Ph.D.
Saint Thomas Church, New York City

✝

New York
OXFORD UNIVERSITY PRESS
1958

Printed in the United States of America

TO CHARLES DUKE

*Friend and true yoke-fellow in the
Lord, who belongs eternally to the
beloved community which is
the theme of this book*

'We shall meet again at Philippi.'

This familiar saying is a mangled misquotation from a grim
dialogue between Brutus and the Ghost in Shakespeare's *Julius
Caesar*. That was to be a meeting in wrath and tears. There
is another kind of meeting at Philippi, which this book tries to
effect: a meeting of God, Christ, Paul, the Christians at
Philippi, and ourselves. May the Holy Spirit
sanctify this meeting to our growth
in the knowledge and love
of God and of one
another.

PREFACE

By general Christian consensus, Paul the Apostle is the greatest Christian who ever lived. Unquestionably he is the greatest in influence. Whether he is greatest in spiritual stature God only knows; but that he is worthy of our reverent regard and diligent study need not be argued.

There are difficulties. It is easy to revere Paul, even to love him; but it is not so easy to like him, and it is not easy to understand him. He is Jewish where we are Gentile, ancient where we are modern, zealous where we are indifferent, paradoxical where we are platitudinous. He has been called, with considerable truth, the innocent father of all heresies. He has suffered this fate because he is not generally a clear expositor of his own convictions. His writing, though profoundly inspired, is seldom easy to read. Both the casual reader and the professional scholar find these difficulties in his writing many and baffling.

We cannot have a real meeting of minds with Paul except by serious effort, but nobody makes this effort without being richly rewarded. In this book we are taking Paul's Letter to the Philippians as our literary portal to his mind and spirit. Among the undisputed Pauline writings it has as good a claim as any to be thoroughly representative of him and to be his simplest—or least difficult—letter. Paul writes from a prison cell, with the shadow of death heavily upon him, but his mood is serene and his mind is calm. His heroic faith and deep love for his Lord and his brethren are nowhere more clearly visible than in this letter. For some readers this commentary may be an introduction to Paul, a first meeting. I hope that it will truly introduce.

Our procedure is the following: each section begins with a translation of the text, and my translation of the Letter as a whole is presented at the close. In the exegesis of each section we try to see what is in Paul's own mind as he writes. Then we consider, in a discursive meditation, what God is communicating to us through Paul's words.

My purpose as a commentator is devotional, but this word needs precise definition. A truly devotional commentary on Holy Scripture must deepen the Christian reader's devotion to his Lord. Its aim is loving knowledge of Him who is the truth. Hence there can be in it no intellectual short-cuts or false simplifications. If I am guilty of any such in this work, my offense is unintended. The purpose of a devotional commentary is to make better Christians out of Christians: to strengthen faith, to enlighten understanding, to quicken love, and to stir up wills. Faith and love are gifts of God, but God gives them to us through other people. A current slang phrase suggests that one person's virtue can 'rub off' on someone else. Thank God, it is true. If something of Paul's vision, courage, joy, faith, and love will 'rub off' on us as we ponder his words to the Philippians, again I say: thanks be to God.

It is a pleasure to acknowledge my debt to my friend Eric W. Hutchison for going over this book with me in its preparation and for many wise and illuminating suggestions.

Carroll E. Simcox

New York
January 1958

CONTENTS

xiii

THEY MET AT PHILIPPI

Chapter One

PAUL THE MAN

He was born Saul of Tarsus. Saul was his Jewish name, but because he was a Roman citizen by birth he had a Latin name also: Paulus. After he became a Christian his Latin name became his common one.

His native city, Tarsus, was essentially a Greek city, though in Paul's time it belonged to the Syrian province of the Roman empire. It was a large city and cosmopolitan, important in both culture and commerce. Though predominantly Gentile, it had a large Jewish community within it. As a seat of Gentile learning it ranked not far below Athens and Alexandria. A keen-minded Jewish boy spending his formative years there must have learned much about the thought and culture of his Gentile neighbors.

We cannot fix the date of his birth. The New Testament evidence in general suggests that he was born a few years later than Jesus. We have no reason to suppose that he ever saw Jesus in the flesh.

His parents were strict Jews, of secure means and social station. Paul was brought up as a Pharisee, with a thorough education in Jewish faith and law. The fact that he learned a trade, that of tent-making, tells us nothing about his family's economic position, for this was the ad-

3

mirable custom of good Jewish families even if they were well-fixed.

Paul had to be converted to Christianity but never to religion as such. From his youth up he was one of those 'incurably religious' souls whose zeal for God makes them fanatics in the eyes of the world. As a Pharisee, he had as his motive and object in all things the search for God's will and the doing of it—all on the assumption that God's will was to be found in the holy Law. As a non-Palestinian Jew, he looked to the famous rabbis at Jerusalem as the experts in this field of knowing God through the Law, and thither he went as a young man to be a pupil of Rabbi Gamaliel the Elder. Gamaliel was a liberal, though soundly orthodox, among the great teaching rabbis of his day. Under Gamaliel's tutelage Paul became an expert interpreter and a zealous practitioner of the legalistic righteousness which Pharisaism represented, and he achieved a considerable reputation for 'blamelessness' in this kind of devotion (Phil. 3:6).

His first reaction to the Christian movement, when he heard of it, was a sense of horror and outrage. Jesus, the leader and hero of the cult, had been crucified—most justly, as Paul saw it—for profaning the holy Law. Paul could see Jesus only as an agent of Satan. There may have been hypocrisy, envy, and fear in the hearts of the men who had contrived the judicial murder of Jesus; but there were many other Jews, Paul among them, who were utterly sincere in regarding Jesus as an enemy of God and of God's people. Hence it was by command of his conscience that he 'persecuted the church of God exceedingly and made havoc of it' (Gal. 1:13).

The account of the conversion that we read in Acts 9 describes the event as something very sudden as well as very dramatic. It must be understood, however, that this shattering crisis event had a background and preparation. This leads us into the realm of psychology, a realm about which we moderns do not know nearly as much as we think we know. Clearly there was some psychological preparation for Paul's conversion, but to say this is to say very little. For the Holy Spirit must work within the psyche, the soul, the inner man. Hence anything that God does with the inner man must appear to us as a 'psychological' phenomenon. It matters little what we call it; but we have a bad habit nowadays of supposing that if the change in a man is 'psychological' it follows that God has had nothing to do with it, that the cause is not divine grace but some frustration or guilt feeling or power drive. Every conversion is psychological in so far as it changes the psyche, the inner man; but its ultimate explanation is theological. This is the Lord's doing.

Paul was present at the trial and execution of Stephen, the first Christian martyr (Acts 6:8-7:60). He saw this glorious young Christian calm before the angry council, with a face 'as the face of an angel.' He heard Stephen's fearless confession of faith in Jesus as the Lord of all, and he looked on as Stephen was stoned to death. He

5

heard Stephen's joyful cry, 'Behold, I see the heavens opened, and the Son of man standing on the right hand of God.' He heard Stephen beg God's forgiveness for his murderers. We wonder what was in Paul's mind during and immediately following this experience. He may have come away from it with some such thought as this:

'These Christians are not simply benighted, deluded, and dangerous enemies of God. They have a bearing, a courage, and a peace which you don't expect to find in such accursed people. Is it of the devil? Or may it be—of God? But if it is of God, how can we make sense of this? How can God endow his most brazen enemies with this peace which passes all understanding?'

It did indeed pass Paul's understanding, but it did not change his mind. Rather it intensified his determination to root out the Christian weed from under the sun. People who can die as Stephen died are dangerous indeed.

The seed of misgiving had been sown, however. His persecuting mania could not blind him utterly to the fact that these followers of the hated Galilean had Something. Furious and frenzied hate can be the sign of a dawning love which the hater is resisting within himself. Paul's final persecuting resolve seems to have been the last desperate spasm of the hate he desperately wanted to keep and which he felt slipping. But this and all other psychological aspects of the conversion, though interesting, are but the human reactions to the divine action. Conversion is the work of the Holy Spirit in the center of man's being. God, not Stephen and other Christians, converted Paul. His was a truly typical conversion. God does the converting, but he uses the faithful witness of his human servants as an authenticating sign, to the soul being converted, of his reality, goodness, and grace.

What happened on the Damascus road is best regarded as the climax of Paul's conversion. He was on his way to Damascus with a warrant from the high priest and council at Jerusalem, authorizing him to arrest any Christians he might find there. His caravan was approaching Damascus when suddenly a dazzling light flooded the party. Paul fell to the ground and heard the Voice saying: 'Saul, Saul, why persecutest thou me? . . . I am Jesus, whom thou persecutest.' The dialogue was private to Jesus and Paul, though the other travelers heard a voice without seeing a man. Paul was temporarily blinded by the light, so he experienced no direct vision of the heavenly Lord. He was directed by the Voice to go on into Damascus, where somebody would meet him and give him further instruction. Paul's submission and obedience opens his new life as a disciple of the Lord whom he had persecuted.

He began his Christian life in Damascus by being baptized. He then spent a time of spiritual preparation and communion with God in a region he calls 'Arabia'—probably not far south of Damascus. This period of preparation corresponds in Paul's life to Christ's season in the wilderness preceding his public ministry. Paul began his work as a Christian missionary worker in Damascus. Three years after his conversion he went to Jerusalem to confer with Peter and the other Christian leaders. It was settled at this conference that Paul should concentrate upon the preaching and ministry to the Gentiles, but the question was far from finally settled at that time. It was to come up as a blazing issue later on.

With all the restless energy of his being Paul threw himself into his apostleship. He toiled for several years in Syria and Cilicia, proclaiming the Gospel of Christ's redemption to Jew and Gentile alike. Then he came to Syrian Antioch, a city of immense importance in the geography of early Christianity. This great city was one of the world's cross-roads commercially and spiritually. It had become a refuge for Christians fleeing from Jerusalem after the martyrdom of Stephen, so Paul found there an established and thriving Christian community, originally Jewish in membership but hospitable to Gentile converts.

It was while working in Antioch that Paul felt moved by the Holy Spirit to go out on his first great missionary journey, which is described in Acts 13 and 14. He was accompanied on this tour by Barnabas and John Mark. It resulted in the establishment of several local churches in southern Asia Minor.

Paul's bold proclamation of the Gospel to Gentiles in this region precipitated the first major crisis in the life of the Church, and this calls for careful examination. If we want to know what got Paul into trouble with his fellow Jewish Christians, we have only to read with some imagina-

tion his sermon in Acts 13:16-41. (This records the substance of Paul's preaching, if not his exact words.) Here is
'the Gospel according to St. Paul.' We find in it an intense
Judaism which believes that 'the God of this people of
Israel chose our fathers' to be his chosen nation; but we find
in it also the clear implication that the salvation of God is
offered through Jesus, the Jewish Son of David, to 'all that
fear God' and 'all that believe.' The 'all' means just that:
Gentiles as well as Jews. When the Jewish Christian leaders
denounced this proclamation, Paul and Barnabas answered
with the fateful words: 'It is necessary that the word of
God should first have been spoken to you: but seeing ye
put it from you, and judge yourselves unworthy of everlasting life, lo, we turn to the Gentiles.' Paul's thesis is that
the promises of God are not simply to Israel but through
Israel to all men. Probably all of the other Jewish Christians would agree to this on principle; but Paul saw no need
to make Jews of the Gentile converts by requiring of them
circumcision and the adoption of the Mosaic Law. When
word reached the strict Jewish Christians at Jerusalem that
Paul was not making Jews of those whom he made Christians, they resolved to silence him or to force him into
conformity.

The issue could not be evaded or postponed, so Paul
and Barnabas went to Jerusalem to have it out with the
leaders there. This meeting is the first great council of the
Church, and can be dated around the year 50. Paul and
Barnabas were charged with heretical teaching and prac-

tice in their refusal to bring Gentile converts under the Law. In their own defense, they pointed to the wonderful fruits of their mission as evidence that God approved and blessed it. They won their case, and the victory is a credit not only to them but to Peter and the other Jerusalem leaders who had to be shown. The decision was that Paul and Barnabas were to carry on their mission as before, but that they were to teach the Gentile brethren to avoid certain practices (Acts 15:20) which were offensive to Jewish propriety. Such was the official decision of the Jerusalem council, but Paul's troubles with Christian Judaizers were by no means at an end. They were to plague him wherever he went to the end of his life.

Paul's subsequent missionary journeys are fully chronicled in Acts, and we need not summarize them in detail. In or around the year 57 he returns to Jerusalem bearing a thank-offering to the 'mother church' at Jerusalem from Gentile converts. On this occasion he is arrested as a disturber of the peace and kept in prison for two years, the first of his two major imprisonments. As a Roman citizen he had the right of appeal to Caesar, which appeal he made, and consequently he was brought to Rome to stand trial in an imperial court. While in Rome he was held in custody for two years before coming to trial. It was during this Roman imprisonment (*c.* 60-62) that he wrote his Letters to *Ephesians*, *Colossians*, and *Philippians*, with the briefer Letters to Philemon and to Timothy (the second Epistle). He may have enjoyed a short period of freedom following this imprisonment, but if so it could not have been for long. The Church's tradition holds that he suffered martyrdom during the Neronian persecution of the year 64.

How shall we assess the man and his work? The latter is easier to evaluate, because it is a matter of clear history. His most lasting and far-reaching contributions may be summarily stated thus:

(1.) By breaking down the wall between Jew and Gentile, Paul made it possible for Christianity to pass from its original form and dimension as a Jewish messiah-cult into a world religion of world redemption. He catholicized and universalized Christianity. Perhaps we should note here that Paul would say, and any Christian would say, that it was Christ, not Paul, who broke down this barrier. But Paul was the effective human instrument of Christ's spiritual conquest of the world.

(2) Paul (again, Christ working through him) demonstrated convincingly that Jesus is not a dead hero who belongs to the past but a living Lord with whom his faithful ones can enter now into a vital union which gives them supernatural strength and eternal life. Paul did not invent this saving reality, of course; he demonstrated it so powerfully and triumphantly in his own life that to this day he stands as a living proof of the truth of this incredible thing.

(3) Paul is the human architect of the Church as a *koinonia*, a fellowship of believers whose human differences are transcended and transformed in their common life in

their common Lord. 'There is neither Jew nor Greek, there is neither bond nor free, there is neither male nor female: for ye are all one in Christ Jesus' (Gal. 3:28).

(4) He was the Church's pioneer theologian, the first Christian of first-rate intellect and training to attempt to think out and to think through the Christian faith. His contribution in this field consists of the kind of preliminary spade-work that is indispensable. Paul wrestled mightily with such theological problems as grace, free-will, forgiveness, justification (the problem of how the most holy God can accept sinful man), atonement (the problem of how Christ by his self-sacrifice can reconcile man to God), Christology (the true relationship of Christ to God and to man), and other such fundamental problems of Christian thought. It is fair to say that he did not solve any of them in such a way that we can consider the case finally closed. What he did—certainly much more than any other Christian thinker of his day—was to get Christian theology started, and along the right lines.

The assessment of Paul the man is more difficult, and also more humanly interesting. It is hard to know where to begin this task, but we might well begin with the dictum of a famous German professor who used to exclaim, in his lectures on Paul: *Aber, meine Herren, dieser Paulus war ein feiner Kerl*. He was a fine fellow, one of God's noblemen. He was a man of intense personal force, unquestionably one of the most effective leaders ever to work in any cause; but his type of leadership is not that which appeals most to the modern democratic taste. He was an irresistible compeller rather than a sweetly reasonable charmer.

Our strictly biographical knowledge of him must be gained by inference from his work, and above all from his own writings. Of course, he is the major hero of the Acts of the Apostles written by St. Luke, an honest and competent historian. In some sections of Acts Luke writes as a first-hand witness, but in others he must rely upon second-hand information and we can never be absolutely sure that he has accurate knowledge of every detail. Among the most conspicuous personal data we may set down the following facts:

Paul was a very cosmopolitan citizen of his Jewish-Roman-Hellenistic world, certainly as compared to his fellow apostles. He was a city man rather than a rustic. (It should be noted in this connection that Christianity was from the first a distinctly urban-proletarian movement, making its greatest appeals to the masses of slaves and workers in the cities. Paganism held out against Christianity most stubbornly in the rural regions.)

About Paul's personal appearance we know nothing. Apparently he was one of those people who must be known in order to be appreciated, who lack the personal magnetism that conquers all at first contact. (The evidence is in his own testimony, in II Cor. 10:10.) He was trilingual, with a working knowledge of Hebrew (both classical and the contemporary Aramaic vernacular), Greek, and

Latin. He thought in Hebrew even as he wrote in Greek. He was intimately familiar with the Jewish scriptures both in Hebrew and in the Greek version known as the Septuagint. He had some knowledge of Gentile Greek literature, as is evidenced by occasional quotations and echoes in his writings. There are very few traces of conscious humor or of the light touch in his writings, but this is no proof that he had no sense of humor.

Among his personal traits certain qualities stand out clearly. He was sensitive and inclined to be quick-tempered (Gal. 5.12 and Acts 13:8-11). He was deeply affectionate, with a dependence upon his friends unusual in a man of his temper. The evidence for this is all over his writings. His mood was mercurial far beyond the average, ranging from deepest melancholy to highest exaltation.

A classical scholar has suggested an apt comparison between Paul and Homer's Odysseus, summed up in Homer's stock epithet for his hero: *polytropos*—'of many wiles,' 'of shrewd devices,' 'infinitely resourceful.' Odysseus is *polytropos* in his steadfast and heroic endeavor to return to his home after the Trojan war. The thought of his beloved Penelope and his home and kingdom sustains him through all trials and losses. Paul is *polytropos* as he agonizes in his labor to bring men to God through Jesus Christ. Hence in both Paul and Odysseus we find the same fiery energy, driving restlessness, captivity to their unfinished work, and heroic transcendence of things past and present as they press on toward the high mark of their calling.

On the evidence, it is reasonable to say that Paul was by nature a neurotic personality, and by super-nature—'in Christ'—a mighty man and a saint. He finds in his own experience of redemption and transformation the sufficient validation of his claim that if any man be in Christ he is a new man. And this explains something about Paul that is bound to puzzle us: his quite shameless pointing to himself as an example of what a Christian ought to be. The conventional preacher of the Gospel, in our day, does not stand in the pulpit and say to us 'be ye followers of me' (I Cor. 4:16). This would be regarded as blatant spiritual egotism. Only a Paul can get away with it. Paul's experience of renewal and change in Christ had been so shattering, so complete, that he could not be reticent about it, and it was far better so. He made it entirely clear that it was all the Lord's doing and none of his own, so his boasting was not of self but of Christ.

We are kept vividly mindful throughout Paul's writings of the paradox that he who, by the grace of God, has labored more abundantly than they all (I Cor. 15:10) is also the chief of sinners (I Tim. 1:15). There is no strictly logical resolution of this paradox. It is simply the solid fact of the regenerate soul. As one grows in Christ one discovers more and more of the dark image of the former man, the old self dying but not yet dead, in the soul of his renewed being. The process of emancipation from sin carries along with it the progressive realization of sin as a lingering residuum of the old self, which is doomed and now dying but still malignantly alive. Hence the acute inner tension between the old and the new, the powers of death and the powers of life, in the soul of Paul the typical Christian. The best metaphor to express this reality is that of the travail of birth. The creation of life, in either the spiritual or the biological realm, is painful. The Peace of God comes with the agony of birth, an agony that must go on until the death of the old man is swallowed up in the final victory when God shall be all in all.

The nature of Christ's victory in Paul will become clearer as we sit down with the Letter and let Paul speak to us.

Chapter Two

THE LETTER

What Paul wrote in the Letter is very much more important than when and where he wrote it and whether or not he wrote it all at one time. These are questions for the professional critics. But no intelligent reader wishes to ignore them, and so a brief consideration of the main points is now in order. We shall note (1) what we know about the Philippian church, (2) what seems most likely as to the place and date of writing, and (3) the question of whether the Letter is a single composition or a piecing together of two letters, both by Paul, written to the Philippians at different times.

Philippi stands out in his memory as the first place where he stayed for long on his first visit to Europe. It was the capital of Macedonia, named after the famous King Philip. Paul associates it with 'the beginning of the Gospel' (4:15) in the Gentile West.

When he came to Philippi on his first visit, around A.D. 52, he found there a Jewish community and he preached to his countrymen. Their place of assembly was an open spot beside a river, and here under the sky he proclaimed the good news of God in Christ. Among his converts was Lydia, who became one of the great ladies of the Church.

17

She was a Gentile God-seeker who had been drawn toward Judaism by the faith and life of the Jews. She proved a valuable and devoted helper of Paul. He stayed long enough in Philippi to establish a church and to get his parishioners firmly grounded in their new faith. His sojourn was ended by the violent incident recorded in Acts 16:14-40.

Five years later Paul returned to find cheering evidence of growth and development. He was able to come again the following year. It is clear that the Philippian church gave him peculiar satisfaction and joy. When some churches were resisting his leadership and even openly defying it, this one remained loyal to him. It further endeared itself by responding generously to his appeal for the relief of the afflicted brethren in Palestine. It was his ideal parish.

So much for the known facts. The first big question about the Letter concerns its place of writing. It could have been either Rome, or Caesarea, or Ephesus. Paul was in prison as he wrote. Caesarea is the least likely possibility. It is very far from Philippi, and the Letter indicates frequent communication at the time between Paul and the Philippians. Ephesus is more plausible. It was a provincial capital and had a praetorium and a staff of 'Caesars servants', thus squaring with certain details in the Letter. Moreover, it was within easy reach of Philippi.

The third alternative is Rome, and both tradition and the evidence give it the strongest claim. Paul's imprisonment there, awaiting trial before the imperial court, was a lengthy one, and the terms of his confinement were such that he could freely communicate with those outside by letter and messenger. As he writes, he seems to have immediately before him a local church situation in which there is much partisan division, moving him to think gratefully of the wonderful unity that prevails in Philippi. The tone of the Letter is that of a man who knows that he may die before long and is cheerfully reconciled to this prospect, while at the same time he hopes that he may be spared for the sake of his work on earth. This would be Paul's state of mind in his Roman imprisonment, when he has no way of knowing how his case will be settled. Another fact strongly supporting Rome appears in verses 12-18 of the first chapter, where he expresses satisfaction in the prospect of a trial that will bring Christianity to the attention of the whole world. Even now his imprisonment is 'known throughout the palace.' To be sure, there were other imperial palaces than that of Rome. But he would hardly have seen so great a strategic propaganda value in a trial in some lesser city. If the case of Paul the accused Christian could become a *cause celebre* in Rome, it would be known henceforth as a movement that even Caesar would have to take seriously. This seems to be in Paul's mind, and it powerfully confirms the traditional view that the Letter was written in Rome.

All things considered, this view is the strongest. Adopting it, we date the Letter between the years 60 and 62.

There is another major critical question, as to whether this is all one letter, written all at once, or an incorporation of two writings of Paul into one document.

The question arises when we note the abrupt change of tone and content at the beginning of chapter 3. Here suddenly is interjected a polemical denunciation of Judaizing 'dogs' and 'evil workers.' This note comes with jarring suddenness and a strong incongruity with its context. The passage in question consists of 3:1b-19. Many critics have concluded that this passage belongs to an earlier writing, and that the keeper of the scrolls in the Philippian church tied it in with the later one, which is the body of the Letter. This is most likely, though it is not a necessary assumption. Paul was a man of moods. He may have written the Letter at several sittings and with no attempt at perfect unity of spirit and uniformity of theme. Such spasmodic thinking and speaking was characteristic of him. Granting this, we shall none the less adopt the critical assumption that this passage is an interpolation from an earlier letter of Paul, which he wrote to the Philippians at a time when the Judaizers were making a serious effort to undermine his work in his absence. It is well to note that whatever opinion we hold on this question makes no real difference to our understanding of the content itself, which is all Paul.

There may still be some critics of the extremely negative school who would say that we have no right to assume that the Letter was actually written by Paul, that this has to be proved. It seems unnecessary to take this objection seriously. The burden of proof surely falls upon the gainsayer in this case. A school of radical German critics of the nineteenth century attacked the Pauline authorship of the Letter almost entirely on the ground that it lacks Paul's usual polemical thunder: therefore it must be by someone else. This is a bit like saying that the Churchill who delivered warlike speeches about Hitler could not have written friendly letters to Roosevelt. Merely to state the case is to see its hollowness. Moreover, there is some polemical thunder in it, as we shall see in due course. If this Letter was not written by Paul, nothing was.

Chapter Three

GRACE AND PEACE TO YOU

1:1-2.

Paul and Timothy, slaves of Jesus Christ, to all the faithful in Christ Jesus who are at Philippi, with the bishops and deacons: grace and peace to you from God our Father and from the Lord Jesus Christ.

The salutation follows the general form of conventional greeting in all ancient letters, but Paul writes his with a Christian difference. His greeting is from Paul and Timothy 'in Christ' to some faraway friends 'in Christ,' and distance disappears in that holy bond. Timothy is with Paul, and the two have talked and thought together about their friends in Philippi. Timothy had helped Paul in the founding of the church and shares fully his loving concern for it. Both men are *slaves of Jesus Christ*, meaning that they belong to him body and soul and consider him their only master.

The Letter is to all the faithful at Philippi: the *hagioi*, usually translated 'saints.' This term can mislead us, with our idea of saints as people far advanced in the life of holiness. In New Testament usage, the saints are simply Christians, living members of Christ and hence partakers of the grace which is sanctifying them.

The *bishops and deacons* are the local church officials. This is in the days before the various orders of the ministry attained sharp delineation. The words mean 'overseers and assistant ministers.'

Grace and peace to you—not from Paul and Timothy, but *from God our Father and from the Lord Jesus Christ.* In purely secular or pagan address it would be something like 'health and prosperity to you' without any reference to the divine giver of all blessing. Paul converts the usual vague expression of good will into a prayer and a benediction. Grace and peace do not just happen to somebody: they must come from God. The linking of *the Lord Jesus Christ* with *God our Father* implies full recognition of the unity of the Father and the Son in their relation to their faithful people.

Timothy is mentioned at the beginning. When the Letter is read aloud to the faithful at Philippi they will know that Timothy shares with Paul his tribulation, his joy, and his devotion to them. Paul wants his young companion and coadjutor to have the recognition he deserves. Paul is Timothy's superior in rank, in years, and in ability, but he stands not at all on that. Both being *slaves of Jesus Christ* there is no real difference or inequality between them.

Differences in rank, endowment, and function there must be in the body of Christ as in the world; but let not my lord bishop suppose that he is more important to God than is the church janitor. If both are *slaves of Jesus*

Christ there are no greater and less. The Master himself enjoins us: 'Ye know that they which are accounted to rule over the Gentiles exercise lordship over them; and their great ones exercise authority upon them. But so shall it not be among you: but whosoever will be great among you, shall be your minister; and whosoever of you will be chiefest, shall be servant of all.' (St. Mark 10:42-44.) This is axiomatic with Paul. Would that it were so with all of Christ's ministers and people!

The bishops and deacons are mentioned in the greeting as if by afterthought. The greeting is not to the ministers and leaders of the church and then to the laity, but to all of them together. This implies no low view of the ministry, for Paul held in fact a very high view of it. But the ministry is seen as a part of the body as a whole, not as something separate and higher.

The Christians at Philippi are *saints*, but they are also sinners. When Paul addresses his fellow Christians as saints he thinks of what they are in process of becoming by God's grace, rather than of what they already are. It is the only realistic way of thinking about any Christian. None of us has arrived at the high mark of our calling in Christ: not even the mighty Paul himself (3:13-14). But if we are faithfully trying and persevering in Christ's way, we are moving toward the glory which shall be revealed in us. The saint is the sinner who is walking in this way.

Grace and peace to you from God our Father and from the Lord Jesus Christ. The grace and peace of God are the two sides of one coin. It is the gift of God, never the achievement of man; and it is the fundamental, constitutive fact of the whole experience of being a Christian. To be in Christ is to know God's gracious favor toward us and to know that we are picked up and carried along on the wings of his grace. Says Thomas à Kempis: 'They travel lightly whom God's grace carries.' How much of this exuberant abounding in grace we find in Paul! To receive grace is to know that we are loved and we are helped, that the God who makes such hard demands on us is all on our side, that he asks nothing of us without enabling us to do it. He calls us to be perfectly Christ-like in all our being and all our doing. The demand is crushing. But along with his demand is given his promise: my grace is sufficient for you; trust me for it, rely absolutely upon it, and *I* will do it for you, in you.

With this grace comes God's peace. It is not what the world calls peace. It is not absence of strife, absence of pain, absence of enemies. It is not even philosophical happiness. The Stoics of old used to debate whether a good and wise man could be happy if stretched out on a rack. An English wag once commented: 'Well, maybe a very good man on a very bad rack!' This question is better pondered in a class-room or over the tea-cups than on a real rack in good working order. But in any case the Stoic's question envisions a peace fundamentally different from the peace of God. The peace of God is that peace with God which is given to him who finds his sole joy in doing God's will.

Paul had no peace with God until he gave himself over to the complete obedience of Christ. Then his peace began—and also his troubles. The peace of God in this world does not provide a happy adjustment to the circumstances of this world. That happy adjustment will come only in heaven. But the real, all-out Christian is content to have it so.

The paradoxical glory of the peace of God is well expressed in the hymn:

> *They cast their nets in Galilee*
> *Just off the hills of brown;*
> *Such happy, simple fisherfolk,*
> *Before the Lord came down.*
>
> *Young John who trimmed the flapping sail*
> *Homeless, in Patmos died.*
> *Peter, who hauled the teeming net,*
> *Head-down was crucified.*
>
> *The peace of God, it is no peace,*
> *But strife closed in the sod.*
> *Yet, brothers, pray for but one thing—*
> *The marvelous peace of God.*[1]

The grace and peace of God come to us through Jesus Christ. Whether we say that it comes from the Father and the Son, or from the Father through the Son, is ultimately immaterial. We cannot know the grace and peace in its reality except as God gives it to us through Christ. To see Christ is to see the Father; to receive from Christ is to receive from the Father.

1. W. A. Percy.

Chapter Four

UNTIL THE DAY

1:3-6.

I thank my God whenever I remember you, and constantly in all my prayers I intercede for you all with joy because of your fellowship with me in the Gospel from the first day to the present. As I do this I am confident of one thing: that he who has begun a good work in you will follow through with it until the day of Jesus Christ.

The recollection of his days in Philippi brings such joy to Paul in his lonely cell that he cannot think of them without thanking God.

His prayers are to *my* God. So much of his time now is spent with God as his only companion that God has become preciously intimate without being his private deity in a selfish and exclusive sense. His prayers to *my* God are for *them.*

What he is most grateful for is their fellowship (*koinonia*) with him in the life and work of the Gospel from the beginning, some ten years before, to the present. He has seen little of them in the flesh, but in this sharing of the Christ-life they do not need to be physically together in order to realize their togetherness and to rejoice in its holy comfort. 'Fellowship' seems a rather anemic translation of *koinonia*, and it is certainly over-used among modern Christians, but it is the best we can do. The root idea of the Greek word is that of sharing, having, and using in common. In the New Testament it means that Christian corporate life and mutual belonging which grows out of the common sharing of Christ and his benefits. It is fellowship with God and with one another in Christ.

As Paul prays for them he is sure of one thing above all: that *he who has begun a good work* in them *will follow through with it until the day of Jesus Christ*. Paul, the founder of the church at Philippi, did not begin it; God began it through him. Paul uses two words that would have a vivid meaning to Gentile Christians with some knowledge of the Greek mystery cults: *enarxamenos*—'has initiated,' and *epitelesei*—'will perfect, complete, carry out, follow through.' In the mysteries, the beginning is initiation and the end is perfection. The life in Christ is the true mystery, the only one in which the initiate has any prospect of being perfected at last, and this for the reason that Paul gives: that it is God himself who perfects what he initiates. The Christian's initiation takes place at his baptism; his perfection is consummated at *the day of Jesus Christ*. This day of the Lord's coming will see the triumphant end of what God is now doing with his people. Paul's view of this day has been modified since his earlier ministry, but not substantially changed. Earlier, he had been sure that he would be alive at the Lord's coming (I Thess. 4:15

and I Cor. 15:51). Now he is not at all sure of this. But the day is still imminent in his mind, and it is the divine climax of all creation. He is confident that when the Lord comes he will find that his people at Philippi have been faithful to the end—and the victory.

I thank my God whenever I remember you. He is little concerned about his own plight. He makes no bid for sympathy. His letter is about them and not about himself, except in so far as his living or dying affects them. Paul is the great apostle, and exemplar, of the freedom which is in Christ. It is freedom from bondage to self, and here we see it. It was said of Elizabeth Barrett Browning that ' 'twas her thinking of others made you think of her.' The same may be said of Paul.

My God. How personal, how private, should a Christian be in his communion with God? We are often reminded that Christ teaches us to pray 'Our Father' rather than 'My Father,' and that even when the Christian prays alone he should say '*Our* Father . . . Give *us* this day . . . Forgive *us our* trespasses . . . ' These pronouns remind him that he is never really alone with God, that he always comes to the Father as one of a family of children. This is true, and always needed. Yet there is a place, a vitally necessary place, for a peculiarly private intimacy with God. It can be private without being selfish or exclusive. Paul, or Peter, or Mary, or you, or your neighbor, is after all a unique individual in God's sight. He loves us not simply all together but one by one, each one for his own sake. God has some things to say to you that he can say to no one else, and the same is true of some things you have to say to God. Much prayer must be strictly private business. Paul's prayer is the prayer that only Paul can offer; and in his lonely cell he knows that he is not alone, for God is there with him, closer than hands and feet. Who will criticize him for saying *my* God?

'I thank my God whenever I remember *you*.' They must have felt a bit sheepish when that was read to them in church. Who were they, that this great giant of a Christian should thank God for *them*? They knew what shambling, clumsy novices in Christ they were. So, in fact, did he. But Paul thanks God for the glory that is beginning to shine in them, for the direction in which they are moving. The true test to apply to any Christian is not 'How good is he?' but 'Is he on the move?' Paul has known these people for ten years. He should be able to see some evidence of growth in grace, and he does. If a pastor has served a parish for ten years and he can see no sign that his regulars are more Christ-like than the day he began, he must know that he has failed. There is no other test of ministerial success.

'Constantly in all my prayers I intercede for you *all* with joy.' Not just for the stalwart pillars and the shining lights, but for those people who give any pastor a head-ache, who are seemingly only names on the church roll. The pastor finds it easy to thank God for some people and to leave some others tactfully unmentioned in his prayers. All Christians in fact face this temptation. How many American Christians prayed for Hitler and Mussolini during the war? How many of us pray for our enemies as well as our friends? Christian concern must embrace everybody. There are people at Philippi who do not measure up to the high standard of the parish. Every one of them is in Paul's mind and heart as he prays. As he reflects upon these individual poor risks in the Christian enterprise he is reminded that he himself leaves much to be desired as a Christian. The blessing of saving humility comes to him who prays for the unlovable and the unadmirable. We cannot hold the other sinner up to God in our prayer without seeing our own sin more clearly, and rejoicing in the great forgiveness which is offered both to him and to us.

Because of your fellowship with me in the Gospel from the first day to the present. We noted in our exegesis that 'fellowship' is a weak translation of the Greek original. What is meant is a participation of Christians in the life and love of God, which becomes theirs in Christ, a participation which knits them together in that 'blest communion, fellowship divine' that we call the communion of saints. To belong to Christ is to belong to one another; to be in Christ is to be together in Christ.

I had a Japanese Christian roommate in seminary, with whom I lived for several months before learning that he had a wife and two small children in Tokyo. He had not seen them for a year and would not see them for two years more. When I asked 'Don't you miss them?' he answered with perfect sincerity, and I think some surprise at my question, 'Oh, no; we are united in Christ.' It satisfied him and them. This is the communion of saints, the fellowship in the Gospel, realized on the deep level. Paul and his beloved Philippians were likewise united in Christ. As he prayed for them far away there was joyful meeting between God, Paul, and them. This thing is as real in fact as it is beautiful in theory to those who go all the way with their self-commitment to Christ. In the fellowship of the Gospel there is no isolation, no separation, no aloneness.

I am confident of one thing: that he who has begun a good work in you will follow through with it until the day of Jesus Christ. No man can even begin to be a good Christian, still less to finish the job. No man can take his own life in hand at all; he can only put it in God's hands. But Jesus Christ makes this possible for him. A man once stood up at a meeting of Alcoholics Anonymous and gave this testimony:

'When I was a young man I received as a gift a most wonderful watch. That watch not only told time perfectly, it had a chronometer on it and it recorded the phases of the moon. It had just about everything except hot and cold running water. But I soon discovered one thing about that watch: when anything went wrong with it, I couldn't fix it myself, and an ordinary watch man couldn't fix it. I had to take it back to its original maker. Then one day it occurred to me that my life was like that watch: a fearfully complicated thing that I couldn't fix when it needed fixing— as it desperately did. The only thing to do was to give it back to its original Maker.'

The story aptly illustrates the truth Paul is declaring. The Christian has put his life in his Maker's hands and he is now in process of being fixed. The process is long, hard, intricate, and painful. It hurts to be changed from what we are into what God is determined to make of us— fully Christ-like persons. It seems to us to take a long, long time. Fifty, sixty, seventy years: that's a long time to be in God's repair shop! Am I really worth all this toil and trouble to the Almighty? What if I die before the job is finished—as in fact I shall, and must? If God wants so much to get this done, why doesn't he do it in a moment and get it over with? Is it good economy to let this whole earthly life be given over simply to the preparation of a finished soul?

Thus the questions come thronging as we reflect upon the Christian mystery of redemption. Such questions are for God to answer to his own satisfaction rather than for us. It must suffice us, as it did Paul, to know that God knows what he is doing. But there is more to reassure us about it than just the spoken promise of God. Spinoza aptly defines joy as 'the passage from a lesser to a greater perfection.' This is a well-established fact of experience. There is no earthly joy comparable to the joy of knowing that, by the wonderful grace of God, we are growing, we

33

are becoming more and more what he wants us to be. He imparts to us some of his own satisfaction in his craftsmanship with us. It is a great day in the school-boy's life when he realizes that he has the multiplication table *mastered*: no more toil, tears, and sweat over that! To be sure, he sees ahead of him huge mountains of mathematical lore still to be scaled; but he is passing from the lesser to the greater perfection, and in the passage he rejoices. So it is with the soul who sees the mountains ahead grow higher and more forbidding, as he sets his face toward his far-off goal of Christ-likeness. How can he possibly finish it? He cannot. But he who began it in him can.

> *So long thy power has blest me, sure it still*
> *Will lead me on*
> *O'er moor and fen, o'er crag and torrent, till*
> *The night is gone.*

Until the day of Jesus Christ. When we have said that this is one of Paul's eschatological terms we have said what is true, but we haven't said very much. All Christianity is eschatological in that it looks toward the day of Jesus Christ, when the kingdoms of this world, in all their being and doing, shall become the kingdom of our Lord. What is this prospect for us as individual persons? St. John gives us the best answer in human language: 'Beloved, now are we the sons of God, and it doth not yet appear what we shall be: but we know that, when he shall appear, we shall be like him; for we shall see him as he is.' (I St. John 3:2.)

34

Of the day of the Lord's coming no man knoweth; but we know what we are to be doing while we wait for it. We are to be co-operating with the Holy Spirit, who is working within us to conform us to Christ. He began this good work in us; he is carrying it on; and he will see it through—if we let him have his way, if we do our best to keep our obtrusive selves out of his way. Then, when the day of Jesus Christ dawns upon us, we shall be found with our faces toward him. Our present part is to keep walking toward the light, not worrying about whether we have the time and the strength to reach it. The time and the strength are God's.

Chapter Five

LOVE AND INTELLIGENCE

1:7-11.

*It is right that I should think this about you all, since
I have you all in my heart as sharers of grace with me, both in
my chains and in my defense and strengthening of the Gospel.
God is my witness that I long for you all in the very heart of
Christ Jesus. I pray above all that your love may increase more
and more, in accurate knowledge and all true discernment, so
that you will approve all things that matter most and you will
be sincere and blameless to the very day of Jesus Christ, filled
with the fruit of that righteousness which comes from Jesus
Christ and is to the glory and praise of God.*

Has he spoken of them more highly than they
deserve? He thinks not. They who have shared so devotedly in his labor and who now feel so keenly his affliction deserve his grateful prayers for them.

He longs for them *in the very heart of Christ Jesus.*
What he means is that his longing for them is the longing of
Christ-in-him for them.

*I pray above all that your love may increase more
and more, in accurate knowledge and all true discernment,
so that you will approve the things that matter most.* Here
is a most important matter in the Christian life. The Chris-

36

tian is constantly tempted to suppose that he does not need to use his head. Isn't it enough to have a soft heart? No, says Paul. A soft heart needs the close-working partnership of a hard head. The Philippians are growing splendidly in love. May this go on and on in them; but as they grow in love may they grow *in accurate knowledge and all true discernment*, so that they will *approve the things that matter most*. It is only as Christians use their heads, with dedicated determination, that they can avoid the fate of well-meaning fools—that of becoming entangled in pious trivialities.

So that *you will be sincere and blameless*. A sincere and blameless Christian is not simply one who means well and does no harm to anybody; he is one who is single-minded and firm-hearted in all that he does for his Lord. Such a Christian is *filled with the fruit of that righteousness which comes from Jesus Christ and is to the glory and praise of God*. The life which is growing in Christ is filled with a positive, robust, fruitful righteousness, not of 'fugitive and cloistered virtue,' which is the mere absence of gross wickedness. The Christian is not only good, but good for something. This righteousness is given to him by Christ, not achieved by himself; and it is *to the glory and praise of God* because this, rather than the glory and praise of the doer, is its motive and object.

We fix our thought upon the great truth that is rather obscurely expressed in these words:

I pray above all that your love may increase more and more, in accurate knowledge and all true discernment, so that you will approve the things that matter most and you will be sincere and blameless to the very day of Jesus Christ, filled with the fruit of that righteousness which comes from Jesus Christ and is to the glory and praise of God.

Paul is making a plea for dedicated intelligence in religion, for loving God with all our minds. And his plea is ever timely and ever most urgently needed. For every Christian's temptation is to stack his brains at the door of the shrine when he comes to his religion. He must think, and think hard, about all his other concerns: this he knows. But his religion is a matter of love, not logic; so his rest in the Lord calls for a mental snooze. Such is the common assumption about Christianity and intelligence. So false is it, and so mischievous, that it calls for careful analysis. What is the relationship between love and intelligence in the Christian religion?

It has been variously said that love is the beginning of all knowledge, all understanding. *Man lernt nichts kennen als was man liebt* (Goethe). Perhaps one can know a thing without love, but never a person. This statement is true; but it makes sense only if one's love is rational, thinking, hard-headed love. If we refuse to think clearly about the true good of our beloved, our love can do no end of harm. So Francis Thompson laments in a poem whose speaker is a man who has ruined a girl with his unthinking love:

> *Ah, the ill that we do in tenderness,*
> *and the hateful horror of love!*
> *It has sent more souls to the unslaked Pit*
> *than it ever will draw above.*
> *I damned you, girl, with my pity, who had*
> *better by far been thwart,*
> *And drave you hard on the track to hell,*
> *because I was gentle of heart.*
>
> (MEMORAT MEMORIA)

The mother who loves her child in such a way that she cannot take him to the dentist is not 'loving' him to any good effect. 'Love' does the work of hate when it refuses to think. Our Lord commands us to love God with all our mind. What can this mean if it does not mean to use our brains to the utmost in our service of God? There is no room in the authentic religion of Christ for sanctified stupidity. Love and truth are joined together by God in a wedlock that no man can put asunder with impunity. Christian love's sole and total object, always, in all things, is truth. When we love another as Christ commands we seek the answer to only one question: what does truth dictate as his ultimate best interest? To love another person intelligently is to ask the answer to that question and to give our all to the realization of it.

 Paul prays that the Philippians may grow in intel-

39

ligence as they grow in love *so that you will approve the
things that matter most*. Only as they love God intelligently
can they see God's priorities, the essentials, the things that
matter most. Otherwise they can only entangle themselves
in things that matter less, or not at all. We all know clergy
whose love for God is deep and genuine, but who are so
preoccupied with ritual niceties, promotional gimmicks,
civic enterprises, and the tricks of their trade, that their
preaching covers virtually every topic except the Gospel.
Some of these lesser things are good and useful in themselves but they are not Christian essentials and they have
crowded out the divine vitalities. The victims of this error
have not grown in Christian good sense. Nor is this an
exclusively clerical failing. Some lay people in every parish
are so busy doing good things with their time and money
that they cannot worship with their brethren, they cannot
pray, they cannot read their Bible, they cannot make a
decent pledge. They lack that awareness of God's priorities which must grow with love if their Christianity is to
be of any use to God, man, or themselves.

Paul's statement that this combination of love and
intelligence makes one *sincere and blameless* may puzzle
us, because we use these two words very carelessly. 'Sincerity' is one of the most talked about virtues. It needs more
thinking about. Everybody seems to be in favor of it, and
everybody thinks he can spot its presence or absence at
a glance. But this is playing God with a vengeance, for
certainly nobody less than God can see and judge any-

body's sincerity. How sincere am I? I doubt that I can answer that question within a mile of the truth, and I am quite sure that my closest friend or my bitterest enemy can come no closer. It would be wiser for us all to chuck this whole foolish enterprise of talking about peoples' sincerity as if we really knew something about it. To be completely sincere is to be completely single-minded in one's allegiance to what he professes. A completely sincere Christian serves his Lord with no thought of self. It may well be that there is not, nor ever has been, a completely sincere Christian under the sun. In any case, Paul is saying that it is only as our love is pure and our thought is clear that we can begin to meet the demands of sincerity.

He prays that they may be both sincere and *blameless*. This word, too, calls for some unwonted reflection. Paul would agree with Milton that we should not praise any fugitive and cloistered virtue whose only merit is that it does no harm. A blameless Christian is one whose performance is not merely not-bad but is positively good. If a totally blameless Christian exists, he not only abstains from evil but he does all good within his power.

In sum: a sincere Christian is one whose whole life is an undivided and unambiguous devotion to the *things that matter most*, the things of Christ; and as he does this he becomes blameless and strong in *that righteousness which comes from Jesus Christ and is to the glory and praise of God*. There is a righteousness—and how much of it there is!—which is to the glory and praise of its doer: as

41

witness the Pharisee in the temple, boasting that he is not as other men are. His righteousness is his own achievement. By a grim paradox it becomes his own damnation since it engenders in him the pride which alienates him from God. The *righteousness which comes from Jesus Christ* is totally different in kind and in consequence because it is totally different in motivation. The Christian's motive is to glorify God by being a faithful follower of Jesus Christ. He knows that in himself dwelleth no good thing, but he hopes that with God's help he can so live in Christ that he may be found at last a good and faithful servant for his Lord's sake and not his own.

Chapter Six

ADVANCEMENT THROUGH ADVERSITY

1:12-14.

I want you to know, brethren, that these things that have happened to me serve for the advancement of the Gospel, since my imprisonment as a Christian is a fact known throughout the whole palace guard and by everybody else; and most of our brethren have been made bolder by it, so that they dare to proclaim the word of God more courageously.

If they suppose that Paul's arrest is a terrible blow to the cause they misunderstand the true state of the case. This is just the lift the Gospel needs at this point: a lift into the limelight of important affairs in the Roman world. The whole palace-guard now knows him, since he is its prisoner; and to know Paul is to hear from him the Gospel of Christ. The men assigned to watching him naturally talk to him about his strange crime of being a Christian, and they talk about it to everybody else. So the question is being fully aired on all sides: who and what are these Christians? What are they up to? Are they dangerous, and if so why? Who is this Christ whom they worship?

Most of the brethren, not all, have taken courage at the news of Paul's imprisonment, and are preaching the

43

proscribed Gospel more boldly and openly now. Here is something one does not expect to find in ordinary circumstances. The ruling powers of a state can normally intimidate the agents of a subversive movement by prosecuting and punishing its leaders. But these Christians are different; at least, many of them are, and when they learn of Paul's imprisonment they grow more audacious, as if they were asking for trouble.

They do this not for Paul's sake but for Christ's. Remembering what the world did to their Master on Calvary, and his warnings that they should receive similar treatment, they realize that Paul's arrest is a sign that the Christians are now on the morn of a decisive battle. So they attack boldly, Paul's imprisonment being the signal to strike. They may have reflected also that the world's persecution of Paul reflects the world's anxious fear of the Christian movement. When the enemy is as nervous as this, strike!

⌐

In this passage we meet that which makes authentic Christianity invincible in action. What the world calls crippling adversity the Christian hails as God-given opportunity. Is Paul a prisoner of the Roman palace-guard? Then thank God! For these soldiers are key-men in the Roman world. They come from everywhere, they go everywhere; and in that militaristic society a soldier is an authority on every subject—including religion. Convert one of them and you gain a follower of great value to the cause.

The soldier's trade is courage. Let him see the courage of a Paul, in prison, under the lash, on the scaffold, and he is bound to ask whence comes this courage that is so much stronger than mere Stoic endurance.

There is no conceivable life situation in which the Christian does not have an opportunity to glorify his Lord before the hostile and unbelieving world. Whatever any sane man may think about Christianity, when he sees a Christian suffering or dying as a victor and not as a victim he must take note that he is seeing Something not of this world. All circumstances, but above all the adverse ones, are made to order for the Christian who wants to bear witness to his crucified Savior. Is he sick? He will offer his sickness to God, and it will be blest and sanctified. Is he poor? He will remember that the King of all creation became a pauper for our sake, and that his saints in being poor make many rich. Is he persecuted? He will forgive his enemies and pray for them. Is he in prison? He will re-member Paul's cheerful and loving ministry to those who caged him. How ridiculous to suppose that the only Christian who can proclaim the glory of the Lord is the healthy, respected, secure man in the pulpit! No pulpit is more strategically effective than a bed of pain, a home in an alley, a cell or a gallows. This is the first principle of Christian evangelism.

Most of the Christians in Rome and elsewhere who knew of Paul's imprisonment were made bold by it because they understood this first principle. They remembered the words of Jesus: Blessed are ye, when men shall revile you, and persecute you, and shall say all manner of evil against you falsely, for my sake. Rejoice, and be exceeding glad: for great is your reward in heaven: for so persecuted they the prophets which were before you.' (St. Matt. 5:11-12.) Christ's reference to the prophets of Israel is a reminder that when the servant of God is really doing his work the world's antagonism comes as a proof that he is on the right track. If you think that you are doing God's will for you, but it all goes so smoothly that the world seems to be happily co-operating with you, the time has come to ask whether you are serving God or yourself. When you are serving God truly, the world is against you, because the world is afraid— seeing in you the Lord's salvation, which it needs and which it shrinks from in terror.

You can help the world to overcome its fear of the Lord by standing fast in your love of the Lord, whatever the world may do to you. Ultimately the world is overcome and brought to God by those whom it hates and hurts for their uncompromising love.

Chapter Seven

PREACHERS SINCERE AND INSINCERE

1:15-18.

Some indeed preach Christ out of envy and rivalry, and others out of genuine good-will; some out of love, knowing that I am placed here because of my defense of the Gospel, while others proclaim Christ out of partisanship, not sincerely, thinking that in this way they will add to my trouble in my confinement. What follows? Christ is preached on all sides, sincerely or insincerely, and so I will rejoice.

Here is the first baffling note in the Letter. How can anybody truly *preach Christ out of envy and rivalry?* The envy has Paul as its object. Are they preaching Christ to spite him? It seems strange, but apparently it is true. These envious and contentious preachers of Christ are partisans who resent Paul's leadership. They are saying, 'Now that Paul is in prison, we'll show him that he isn't the only one who can preach the Gospel.' This is the most charitable construction to put on their motives, which we can only guess at. Paul imputes a lower motive to them in his assertion that they preach *not sincerely, thinking that in this way they will add to my trouble in my confinement.* We like to think that he was wrong, but we must remember that he knew them and we do not.

Whatever their motives, he rejoices that *Christ is preached on all sides, either sincerely or insincerely.* We are puzzled, for we should think that he would be gravely concerned about any possible insincere preaching of the Gospel for which he is laying down his own life. But what is uppermost in his mind is the realization that the divine commission is being carried out by others than himself; therefore he can face whatever lies ahead with the assurance that the proclamation of the Gospel does not live or die with him.

And so I will rejoice. He is determined to suppress his feelings of resentment and fix his mind only on the progress of the Gospel in the world.

✒

For the reasons just noted, we are puzzled by Paul's apparent indifference to the motives of others in preaching the Gospel. But two facts stand out clearly, and they are as relevant today as they were then. The first is that the preaching of Christ to the world is never one man's business, but the corporate business of the whole Church. The second is that people do not have to be perfect saints if they are to preach and witness to Christ. If that were requisite there would be no preaching.

Consider this second point first. Very often, when nice or un-nice things are being said about a clergyman, he is praised as 'sincere' or damned as 'insincere.' As we noted in an earlier chapter, this easy talk about sincerity is a bad habit of ours. Only God can know anybody's sincerity or in-sincerity. This good man who preaches the Gospel is not absolutely simon-pure in his sincerity. He cannot be, since he is still a sinner. Grant that he loves the Lord and wants others to love him. That much of him is sincere. But he wants also to be admired for his eloquence, his wisdom, his charm, and he wants people to treat him well. This self-regard ought not to be in him, but there it is. We must trust the judgment of God to judge it and the grace of God to correct it, for we cannot do either. The Gospel is preached by him despite his unworthiness, and God reaches sinners through this sinner. This is the unending miracle of Christian preaching, that it is for sinners only and it is done by sinners only.

It is sad when a Christian, cleric or layman, is motivated in his Christian witness by self-seeking or by partisan bigotry. But this is seldom, if ever, his sole motive. He has a better and holier reason. People who will not be taught and helped by a Christian unless he is 'absolutely sincere' according to their own ignorantly cocksure judgment of his sincerity do not really want to be taught or helped.

The other important truth which Paul declares here is that the preaching of Christ to the world is not one man's business but the whole Church's business. When he hears that others are preaching boldly and openly he real-izes that he himself is no longer indispensable to the Christian movement and he is ready to depart this world in peace. Up to this time, Paul has had very good reason to regard himself as indispensable. Now that others are taking up his tools and his task he can stop worrying about the future of the Gospel.

In many a modern parish we hear the complaint that a little clique, the pastor and a few others, run things as if they owned the parish. In such cases the charge is usually true, but the plaintiffs are the real guilty ones. A Christian parish ought to be so full of people working day and night at their witnessing to Christ, by thought, word, and deed, that they all become indispensable. In that happy case, any one member can be happy and content knowing that the voice of prophecy and the hand of service in his parish will not die with him. The Church is the Church only when it is the community of the concerned, not a clique of the concerned dwelling amidst a family of grumblers and idlers who say that they leave this business to the people who 'think they own the parish.'

Chapter Eight

JOB AND PAUL

1:19-20.

Yea, I rejoice in this, for I know that 'this will turn out to be my salvation' through your prayer and through the supplying of the Spirit of Jesus Christ. I hope and I am sure that I shall not be put to shame, but that with full courage, now as always, Christ will be glorified in my body, whether I live or die.

The words in quotation marks are from Job 13:16.

Paul is counting on two things to see him through: the prayers of his friends, and *the supplying of the Spirit of Jesus Christ.* By linking these two blessings in this way, he is reminding them of what they should pray for above all else—that the Lord will plenteously supply him with this Spirit. If he has this in him, he need have no doubt of his own self in the hour of trial: Christ will be glorified in him, whether he is set free or is condemned to death.

✦

Paul in his prison recalls Job in his affliction. Both men suffer much unmerited pain, both are men of deep faith. But Job is bitterly perplexed by the evil things that have come upon him in the good God's world. He sees in his distresses none of the God-given opportunities to serve and glorify God which Paul sees, embraces, and uses so joyfully. What makes the difference between the two faithful sufferers? Only one thing, but it makes an infinite difference: the cross of Jesus Christ.

Paul sees God himself taking the pain of the world as his own. Job sees God sitting, serene and untouched, above the water-floods of woe. And this, to him, is the scandal and the perplexity. If God, yea, *since* God is good, just, and all-powerful, why does he let his faithful children fall into such terrible pits of disaster? This is Job's question, to which he finds no answer. Paul does not even ask the question and he does not hunger for the answer. He has reflected upon the mystery, but because he sees God in Christ, coming into the pain of our flesh to redeem it, he is concerned with making use of his tribulations for the extension of God's victory rather than with reconciling the fact of evil with the fact of God's goodness.

How Christians view this mystery is more easily illustrated than defined. A Swiss-French pastor imprisoned by the Nazis recalls his spiritual reaction to the evil situation thus: 'I was not able to stand firm except by remembering every day that the Gestapo was the hand of God—the left hand. The worst of tyrants and the last of cowards will only end by accomplishing Christ's will.'

It is by this faith that Christianity conquered from

the beginning. 'Christianity refused all Epicureanism,' as Friedrich von Hügel observes, 'since man cannot find his deepest by fleeing from pain and suffering, and by seeking pleasure and pleasures, however dainty and refined. And it refused all Stoicism—since pain, suffering, evil are not fancies and prejudices, but real, very real; and since man's greatest action and disposition is not self-sufficingness or aloofness, but self-donation and love. Christianity refused these theories, not by means of another theory of its own, but simply by exhibiting a Life and lives—the Life of the Crucified, and lives which continually relive, in their endless various lesser degrees and ways, such a combination of gain in living and of joy in suffering. Christianity thus gave to souls the faith and strength to grasp life's nettle. . . . It pointed to Jesus with the terror of death upon Him in Gethsemane; with a cry of desolation upon the Cross on Calvary; it allowed the soul, it encouraged the soul to sob itself out. It not only taught men frankly to face and to recognize physical and mental pain, death, and all other, especially all moral evils and sufferings as very real; it actually showed men the presence and gravity of a host of pains, evils and miseries which they had, up to then, quite ignored or at least greatly minimized. And yet, with all this—in spite of all such material for despair, the final note of Christianity was, and is still, one of trust, of love, of transcendent joy.'[1]

Paul wanted his friends to pray that he might

1. (von Hügel, *Essays and Addresses: First Series.* 111–12.)

re-live the Life of the Crucified in his own flesh. The *supplying of the Spirit of Jesus Christ* would make it possible for him so to suffer that the world would see Christ, crucified and risen, in him, as the world's hope of glory. The Christian life is identification with Christ. No other way of conceiving of it is adequate. As Christ suffered, so his living member suffers; as Christ died, so he dies; as Christ rises, so he rises. On Easter Day of the year 362, St. Gregory of Nazianzus preached a sermon to his townsfolk in which he went to the heart of the Christian mystery of salvation. He said:

'Yesterday the Lamb was slain and the door-posts were anointed, and Egypt bewailed her firstborn, and the Destroyer passed us over, and the Seal was dreadful and reverend, and we were walled in with the Precious Blood. Today we have clean escaped from Egypt and from Pharaoh; and there is none to hinder us from keeping a feast to the Lord our God—the feast of our departure . . . Yesterday I was crucified with him; yesterday I was buried with him; today I rise with him. But let us offer to him who suffered and rose again for us . . . Let us offer ourselves . . . Let us know the power of the Mystery, and for what Christ died.' The language of this Easter homily is to us strange and archaic, but the substance of it is the very heart of true Christianity: the Christian's sharing in the suffering, the defeat, and the victory of Christ, in his own body.

There is no way to the resurrection victory except through Calvary. God's 'most dear Son went not up to joy but first he suffered pain, and entered not into glory before he was crucified.'[2] The servant is not greater than his Lord. But to the soul in Christ, the very sharpness of the pain suffered for his sake is proof to the happy warrior that he is on his way to the glory which shall be revealed in him. As one of the early martyrs was being led to the arena he cried: 'Now I begin to be a disciple.' To him, it meant that he was really arriving, after many years of comparative ease and peace which could be counted only as preparation for the real thing: that identification with Christ in his Calvary which is the birth-travail of the life eternal.

[2] (Collect for the Monday before Easter, *Book of Common Prayer*).

Chapter Nine

TO LIVE IS CHRIST, TO DIE IS GAIN

1:21-26.

For me to live is Christ, and to die is gain. But if I live in the flesh, this is fruit of labor for me—and which course I shall take I do not know. I am torn between two desires: the desire to go and to be with Christ, which is much better for me, and the desire to stay in the flesh, which is better for you. Because I am convinced of this, I expect to stay on with you all, for your progress and joy in the faith. Thus your pride in me may abound in Christ Jesus, because of my coming back to you.

Life in the flesh is 'Christ' for him, because his life is wholly surrendered to the service of Christ. If he dies, this will continue; but by death he will enter a closer union with his Lord.

What follows is in broken language but the sense is clear. *Fruit of labor* means fruitful labor. He has this to look forward to if his life is spared. *Which course I shall take I do not know.* He is not implying that the choice is his and that he hasn't yet made up his mind about it. God will decide the issue. But in the next two sentences he expresses his own opinion: God will leave him on earth for a

56

while longer for their continuing *progress and joy in the faith*.

Thus your pride in me may abound in Christ Jesus, because of my coming back to you. This is said in a playful spirit. They are proud of him in the way that any congregation is proud of a good pastor. He does not reprove them for this, but by the curious construction of his sentence he reminds them that their real pride is in Christ rather than in him. When he comes again to Philippi they will all enjoy a delightful feast of mutual admiration—they glorying in him and he in them.

↦

Paul's dilemma as he ponders life and death is the dilemma of any good Christian. *To die is gain* to one's own self, since it means entering more fully into the joy and presence of the Lord. Whatever may await us beyond death, Christ is there waiting to receive his faithful servant and to lead him into the perfected love and higher service of heaven. But what of those here on earth who need us? To be sure, nobody is indispensable, and one must beware of the presumption that God cannot take care of his own without our help. Even so, if we have a loving concern for those whom God is presently caring for through us, we must feel as Paul did: 'They need me here.'

Paul was sure that his life on earth would be prolonged for the sake of those who needed him. He was wrong. Though he may have lived for two or three years after writing this, he died in Rome without returning to Philippi. Even he could go wrong on this calculation, and so can we. It is not for us to say that God will not take us from this world simply because he has work for us here to do. Who are we to know what God will do about the needs of those who need us? Who are we to know even what their needs are? The logic of our faith requires that we be happily content to leave it all in God's hands. Paul had this faith profoundly, but at this moment he was not following the logic of his faith. His reasoning is faulty while his motivation is faultless. It is for their *progress and joy in the faith* that he expects to be restored to them. Their progress and joy have certainly depended upon his ministry up till now, and it is out of sheer devotion to his task that he wants to remain at it. But we trust that he changed his mind once it became clear that he was soon *to go and to be with Christ*. Their progress and joy in the faith had reached the point where it would be furthered by his absence. It was expedient for them that he go away.

Likewise it is often expedient for those who need us that we go away. Sometimes we quarrel bitterly with God's decree. 'What? Expedient for these three small children that their mother should die when they need her most? That a Lincoln should die just when his war-torn nation needs him most? That the only doctor in a frontier community should die when an epidemic is raging? How can we say that such ghastly losses are expedient for anybody?'

In all such situations our faith in God's wise and loving control of things in severely tested. But faith's word is finally this: that there is only one competent judge of what is expedient for us, and that is God, who sees all even as he makes all things work together for good to them that love him.

Chapter Ten

THE PRIVILEGE OF SUFFERING FOR HIM

1:27-30.

Only live worthily of the Gospel of Christ, regardless of whether I come to see you or must be content with hearing about you. Stand in the Spirit, being all of one mind as you fight together for the faith of the Gospel, and don't be afraid of your enemies in any issue. This will be a clear sign to them, from God, of their destruction and of your salvation. For to you is given the privilege not simply of believing in Christ but of suffering for him, waging the same conflict which you saw me fight and you hear that I am now fighting.

What we have translated as *live worthily* means in the Greek 'live worthily as citizens.' The verb emphasizes the Greek idea that good living means good citizenship and does not simply include it as one of the duties of a good man. Aristotle's definition of man as a political animal is entirely congenial to Paul the Jewish Christian, for this concept of man is equally vital to the Hebrew mind. To *live worthily of the Gospel of Christ* is to be a good citizen of the city of salvation, the Church. This thought is uppermost in Paul's mind, but he is thinking also of the duty of the Philippians toward their secular society. Loyalty to the state, civic righteousness, is a necessary implicate of the Christian's citizenship in the kingdom of God. He has the 'divine right of disobedience' against the civil power only when that power is clearly against God's order.

Stand in the Spirit. The Holy Spirit is here seen as the divine strengthening and stabilizing force enabling the Christian to stand up against all adversities.

This will be a clear sign to them, from God, of their destruction and of your salvation. Their adversaries will see that they are fighting against God when they encounter the indomitable courage of the Christians standing in the Spirit, for the Christians are armed from above and so are invincible.

For to you is given the privilege not simply of believing in Christ but of suffering for him. They have seen Paul suffer for his faith. When a Christian thus suffers, it is because he has passed beyond the stage of simple believing in Christ and has entered the higher state of active service as Christ's agent and deputy. The privilege of suffering for Christ is the privilege of doing the kind of work for him that is important enough to merit the world's counter-attack. The sufferer can rejoice in the realization that God now accepts him, not simply as a beloved child, but as a mature son now ready to take an active share in the Father's business on earth.

IGNORED!

The privilege of suffering for Christ's sake. There is no suggestion here that the Christian is to go out of his way looking for trouble. He will get plenty of it, without stirring out of his tracks, when he begins to *stand in the Spirit* and to do battle with the world, the flesh, and the devil in Christ's name.

There are two distinct stages of Christian discipleship. In the first stage, we believe and accept Christ and are accepted by him. The purpose of this stage is to prepare us for the second. In the second stage we become not simply beneficiaries of Christ's love for us but soldiers and servants of that love for others; and now the suffering comes, the labor and the wounds. Its coming is proof that God now accepts us as his grown-up children ready for grown-up work. This is the privilege of suffering for Christ's sake. Its dignity and its complement consist in the fact that Christ is making us active partners with him in his continuing travail for the redemption of the world. If our love for God is Christ-like, we experience a deep satisfaction in doing for him the kind of work that brings upon us pain and cost. He thinks we are ready to take it! He trusts us with burdens which only grown-up souls can bear. Thus we become partners in Christ's own pain. William Blake was one of these grown-up Christians, and he expresses the privilege in these lines:

> *Can I see another's woe*
> *And not be in sorrow too?*
> *Can I see another's grief*
> *And not seek for kind relief?*

> *No! No! never can it be,*
> *Never, never can it be.*
> *Think not thou canst sigh a sigh,*
> *And thy Maker is not by.*
> *Think not thou canst weep a tear*
> *And thy Maker is not near.*
> *O! He gives to us His joy*
> *That our grief He may destroy.*
> *Till our grief is past and gone,*
> *He doth sit by us, and moan.*

The child-like simplicity of Blake's Christ-mysticism should not deceive us. His is the authentically Christian experience of sharing the life and victory of Christ by sharing the redemptive suffering of Christ in the travail of the present moment. The assurance that we are with God and he with us in the pain we suffer for his sake is the privilege of intimate sharing in the very heart of God.

Our Lord's most scornful remembered words were those spoken to his brothers who did not believe in him: 'The world cannot hate you.' (St. John 7:7.) The world *cannot* hate *you*, for you are not worth its hate! A person can enjoy an untroubled existence in this world for the simple reason that he is beneath the world's hate. There is comfort in this, but no privilege, as John Stuart Mill suggested in his saying that it is better to be a man dissatisfied than a pig satisfied, better to be a Socrates dissatisfied than a fool satisfied. It is only as a man begins to measure up to his calling to serve God rather than himself that he suffers the world's opposition.

In Paul's day this opposition usually came in the form of violent hatred and abuse by the world. The name 'Christian' had a sinister and ugly sound, evoking images of cannibalism, incest, morbid misanthropy, and atheism. These were in fact some of the charges against the Christians, and intelligent people believed them. The world's hatred was that of the average decent man when he hears of something vile and revolting to him.

As times and circumstances change the forms of the world's hostility to Christianity change, and the taunts and the charges change. A fighting Christian of our world today will not be charged with atheism or incest, but rather with imbecility, or meddling, or foolish idealism, or sentimentalism, or reactionary conservatism, or revolutionary radicalism. The opposition need not be active or ferocious. It may take the form of ridicule, scorn, patronizing pity, or simple indifference. And it may come from one's fellow Christians. When young Albert Schweitzer resolved to go to Africa on his mad mission of healing love, good Christians in Europe refused to help him; some because they didn't like his theology and others because they thought he was visionary. He was not persecuted, he was shrugged off—a more painful suffering.

But in whatever form the suffering comes, the privilege remains the same. It is the privilege of knowing that God takes you seriously enough to give you an adult's work to do.

64

Chapter Eleven

'OTHERING' YOURSELF

11:1-4.

If then you find any help in Christ, any stimulus of love, any fellowship of the Spirit, any mercy and kindness toward you, make my joy complete by having this same thought and love and mind toward one another. Have just one object: that nothing shall be done out of ill-temper or egotism, and that everything shall be done in true humility, each one of you considering others ahead of himself and seeking their welfare rather than his own.

We are here translating more freely than usual, since a literal rendering of some of Paul's terms would obscure their meaning.

Help in Christ is the experience of having Christ with us and helping us, and the Philippians already rejoice and abound in this experience.

Any stimulus of love. The sense of Christ's love for us stimulates our love for others. We can love others truly only as we know how God loves us.

Any fellowship (koinonia) of the Spirit. On the meaning of *koinonia* see pages 27-28 *supra*. Here, as everywhere in Paul's writings, the Holy Spirit is seen as the divine cohesive force within the Church, drawing and knitting Christians together in one holy bond of charity and mutual concern.

Any mercy and kindness toward you: that is, from God. They experience the mercy and kindness of Christ toward themselves; they are to give to others what they have received from the Lord.

They will make his joy complete by exhibiting the heavenly unity which he now goes on to describe.

But how can such unity be achieved by selfish, sinful men? There is only one way: by surrendering their own spirits to the Spirit of Christ. This involves the rejection of all motives of malice and self-seeking. Instead of trying to climb over his brethren on his way to his selfish goal, the Christian has another goal and another way of working—*seeking their welfare rather than his own*. When John helps Peter instead of John, and Peter helps John instead of Peter, God's kingdom comes on earth as it is in heaven.

~

Why do we love other people—if we do? It is generally agreed among us, whether we are Christians or not, that we ought to love others. The question of why or how we are to love them is very much more of a question.

In commenting upon the general unlovableness of Sherwood Anderson's literary characters, Lionel Trilling offers this curious reason for loving people in literature and in life: 'We do not love people for their essence or their souls, but for their having a certain body, or wit, or idiom, certain specific relationships with things and other people, and for a dependable continuity of existence: we love them for being there.'[1] This is a strange judgment. Does not the obnoxious person stimulate our hate by his crime of 'being there'? It seems that Dr. Trilling is talking here about what makes people interesting rather than what makes them lovable.

Jeremy Taylor brings us closer to the Christian reason for loving others in this mystical analysis of the matter: 'God is in every created being or thing: be cruel towards none, neither abuse any by intemperance. Remember, then, the creatures, and every member of thy own body, as one of the lesser cabinets and receptacles of God. They are what God hath blessed with His presence, hallowed by His touch, and separated from unholy use, by making them to belong to His dwelling.' This is very moving and beautiful, but it requires of us a mystical vision of God in all creatures which few possess.

St. Catherine of Siena brings us much closer to the primary Christian motive for loving others with this reasoning: 'The reason why God's servants love creatures so much is that they see how much Christ loves them, and it is one of the properties of love to love what is loved by the person we love.' This statement is entirely true; but we see how much Christ loves those others only as we realize, first, how

---

1. Lionel Trilling, *The Liberal Imagination*, New York, 1950, p. 41. By permission of Viking Press, publishers.

much he loves us, ourselves. It is in this realization that all Christian loving others begins. Christ so loves us that he completely 'others' himself for us, taking our very life, with all its weakness and mortality and pain and even its guilt, upon himself. When the reality of this truly possesses and captivates us, the *stimulus* of his love for us, *his mercy and kindness* toward us, as Paul puts it, moves us to 'other-ourselves' for others as a continuation of Christ's 'othering-himself' for us.

Chapter Twelve

KENOSIS

11:5-11.

Have in yourselves this mind which is also in Christ Jesus, who, being in form of God, did not consider it any over-reaching of himself to be equal with God; yet he emptied himself, took the form of a slave, and was born in likeness of men. And being found in appearance as man he humbled himself, becoming subject to death—death by a cross. For this reason God has exalted him preeminently, and has honored him with the Name above every name, so that in the Name of Jesus every knee should bow, of creatures in heaven and on earth and under the earth, and every tongue should confess, to the glory of God the Father, that Jesus Christ is Lord.

No other passage so eloquently expresses Paul's conception of the being of Christ, and because it is so fundamental for all Christian thinking about Christ we must analyze it very carefully.

We shall speak of it by its familiar title of the kenosis passage, from the Greek verb in the phrase *he emptied himself*.

Paul asserts that Christ, being eternal God, became man absolutely and completely. He asserts further that in doing this Christ laid aside all of what men would call his eternal dignity and honor as God. He takes upon himself, in the Incarnation, what we men would naturally call a life of indignity, shame, and weakness. But now that *God has exalted him pre-eminently, and has honored him with the Name* (of Lord) *which is above every name* we understand that we were utterly wrong in our original way of thinking about dignity, honor, and power. What we thought was weakness is proclaimed by God himself as ultimate, perfect power and glory.

This certainly is one of the major meanings of the kenosis passage, perhaps the chief. But Paul's description of the Incarnation, indeed the Incarnation itself, raises a vast question that Paul does not try to answer. It is this: in becoming man, does Christ cease to possess the power and knowledge of God, at least for the time of his incarnate life?

Those who hold the extreme kenotic theory say that he did. In this case, the only knowledge and power which Christ possessed during his incarnate life were those of an ordinary man. Needless to say, this collides with the testimony of the Gospels and the faith of the Church. In the Gospels Christ is portrayed as one who 'knew what was in man' (St. John 2:25) and who knew many things that the wisest man cannot learn from strictly human experience. And the Christ of the Gospels manifests superhuman power as well as knowledge. At the same time, the Gospel evidence indicates that Christ had to grow in knowledge and wisdom as any man must. Where such growth is necessary, it is clear, *ex hypothesi*, that the learner does not know everything from the start.

The Church historically has believed and taught that Christ had divine knowledge and power concerning all things involved in his saving mission to the world. Either this knowledge and power were innate in him or the Father supplied them directly, according to Christ's need for them at any given moment.

The question remains forever unanswerable in strictly rational terms. How can the Son of God become true man while remaining true God? Paul does not offer an answer to this question, here or elsewhere. In this kenosis passage he uses the language of poetry, specifically the language of adoration, rather than the language of formal theology.

Some scholars argue very cogently that this is a primitive Christian hymn which Paul quotes, with perhaps some verbal alteration. There can be no doubt that it expresses the earliest Christian belief about Christ in his humiliation and exaltation.

Have in yourselves this mind which is also in Christ Jesus: the mind of self-effacing love.

Who, being in form of God, did not consider it any over-reaching himself to be equal with God. Christ in his eternal being is God; hence it would not be any over-reaching of himself to claim divine dignity and honor since this is already his. But he stands not on this because he has a totally different *mind* in himself: the mind to give rather than the mind to take. This mind is manifested in what he did when *he emptied himself, took the form of a slave, and was born in likeness of men*. He *emptied himself* of all his prerogatives as God. It is an extremely, drastically, strong word to apply to Christ's disposal of his divine powers in becoming man. As Paul uses the same verb elsewhere (I Cor. 1:17, 9:15, and Romans 4:14) it means to make void, to invalidate. We should not press the word as he uses it here to a purely logical end, for Paul is using the language of adoring love to celebrate Christ's love for us, so dramatically revealed in this self-impoverishment for our sake.

In taking on himself *the form of a slave* Christ becomes in fact a slave to men. What makes this so impressive it that it is voluntary and done out of pure love for those whom he comes to serve. Yet in becoming slave he does not cease to be master. Through his self-enslavement to us he seeks to make us slaves to himself: slaves of love answering and responding to his love for us.

He was *born*. Christ as God is eternal, but as man he comes into being at a definite moment in time. Prior to this moment, Christ has no existence as man. Once he has become man he remains man forever, not by ceasing to be God but by carrying his manhood up into his Godhead. God is, henceforth and forever, man in the person of Christ. This is fully implied by Paul in this passage, and we should note this profoundly important truth: that Christ not only gives up something in the Incarnation—his divine dignity; he takes on something—our humanity, which is his forever.

And being found in appearance as man he humbled himself, becoming subject to death. The *appearance* is no illusion. Christ's manhood is real. In appearing to us as man he appears as he truly is. If we had no other proof of this, the fact of his death would be enough. God as God cannot die. God become man can die; and if his manhood is genuine he must. He dies, moreover, the vilest and cruelest death man can suffer: *death by a cross*. The peculiar enormity of this mode of dying is noted by Cicero: 'How shall I describe crucifixion? No adequate word can be found to describe so execrable an enormity.' (*In Verrem*, 5.66.) The idea of a true God who is capable of dying is blasphemous to the Jew and fantastic nonsense to the Greek. As Paul sees it, Christ's self-subjection to death is a mighty achievement which only a divine power and goodness could accomplish. *Death by a cross*: this peculiarly ignominious form of death has been achieved by Christ. What further proof is needed of his real divinity?

For this reason God has exalted him pre-eminently. God the Father shares, absolutely, the love of the Son which pours itself out in such lavish measure—to its own death—for the sake of the beloved; for Christ's love for us is the Father's love for us. A small child once heard the story of the death of Christ very movingly told on Good Friday, and suddenly he burst into tears and exclaimed 'I love Jesus, but I hate God!' The preacher had somehow failed to make the all-important point that 'God' was not detached from the agony of 'Jesus': in all of the Son's afflictions the Father is afflicted. There is one love of God and one passion of God; and Father, Son, and Holy Spirit are all at one in it. The Father manifests his joy in the Son's heroic sacrifice by *exalting him pre-eminently*. In his eternal being, Christ sits at the right hand of the Father; and in his resurrection victory, before he ascends into heaven, this glory of his is openly disclosed to the eyes of men so that we see it as an exaltation by God—his recognition, vindication, and reward of his beloved Son.

And has honored him with the Name above every name. In ancient Hebrew thought, the name of a person is much more than a mere identification tag. The person himself is in his name. The exaltation of Christ's Name *above every name* is the establishment of his supreme lordship over all creatures, however revered and glorious their own names may be.

That in the Name of Jesus every knee should bow. Literally, 'in' the Name. By the use of this preposition Paul clearly means something very much more important than any mere ritual act of genuflecting at the mention of the Name of Jesus. He means that all who see Jesus as he truly is, the sovereign Lord of all creation, will bow to him not only with their knees but in their hearts and lives, in utter obeisance to him. The phrases *every knee shall bow* and *every tongue shall confess* are quoted from Isaiah 45:23: 'As I am God, and God alone, I swear by myself, I swear a

true word, never to be recalled, that every knee shall bow
to me, and every tongue swear loyalty.' The verse is quoted
also in Romans 14: 11, where the reference is to the worship
of God. The homage which Jesus shall receive is that due
to God alone.

*And every tongue shall confess, to the glory of God
the Father, that Jesus Christ is Lord.* Now, at the end of the
hymn, the glorious new Name which Jesus receives in his
exaltation is declared: *Lord.* 'Jesus is Lord' is most probably
the first Christian creed and the ancestor of all later creedal
formulations of the faith. It is the heart and center of any
creed which is truly Christian. We may assume that when
the Philippians were baptized they bound themselves forever to Christ by confessing 'Jesus is Lord.' By this the early
Christian declared his conviction that Jesus is supreme and
sovereign ruler of all creation. He is this, now and forever,
to the glory of the Father who has committed this universal
lordship to him.

Nietzsche hated Christianity, but he hated it with
some discernment; and this passage from his *Beyond Good
and Evil* is entirely true: 'Modern men, with their obtuse-
ness as regards all Christian nomenclature, have no longer
the sense for the terribly superlative conception which was
implied to an antique taste by the paradox of the formula,
"God on the Cross." Hitherto there had never and nowhere

75

been such boldness in inversion, nor anything at once so dreadful, questioning, and questionable as this formula: it promised a transvaluation of all ancient values.'

Before Christ, every intelligent man thought he knew what true power is, true goodness, true wisdom, true love. Hence everybody who believed that God is perfect in power, goodness, wisdom, and love was sure he knew what God must be like in his being and doing. Christ came and turned all that upside down. His Gospel is the transvaluation of all the accepted values. The King of all creation is born in a barn and dies on a cross.

In the great kenosis hymn, Paul glories in this humiliation of God. His glorification of the crucified Saviour must appear as a pathological case to anybody who holds the 'civilized' ideas of God. The God who empties himself, beggars himself, becomes a slave, and dies on a cross is a shocking contradiction of all that we naturally mean by all-mighty, all-glorious, all-wise. Is not power judged by its ability to stay in power? Is not glory judged by its glittering majesty? Is not goodness judged by its abhorring separation from evil? Is not justice judged by its cool judicial detachment from the evil-doer, so that it can judge and condemn evil with the authority of its own pure non-involvement with sinners? Why, of course!

But see what we have here in this wild new Gospel: its Christ, supposedly all-powerful, becomes a helpless babe born of a girl in a stable. He the supposedly all-glorious becomes a slave in rags, whom beggars spit upon as he carries his cross to Golgotha. He the supposedly all-good and all-holy appears as the bosom companion of taxgrafters, prostitutes, tramps, and drunkards. He the supposedly all-just, the judge of all men and nations, lets himself be done to death —the judge going to the gallows for the condemned. If this fantastic tale is true, the whole world is wrong. Are these Christians trying to tell us that they are sane and that the rest of the planet is crazy?

One thing should be clear enough. Christianity is not a religion among the great religions of the world—one of them, one with them in their major premises. We are fond of saying in our day that Christianity, Islam, Buddhism, Judaism, Hinduism, and all other major religions have a great deal in common, that their differences are after all quite secondary. This may be granted—if we can put into the secondary category the small matter of what one believes God is like. The God of the Christian is totally unlike the God of anybody else. The 'religions of the world' are of the world indeed, insofar as they proclaim to the world gods acceptable to good sense, to civilization, to culture, to law and order. The God of Jesus Christ is utterly incompatible with these other gods.

Christ said that he came not to condemn the world but to save it. True enough; but there is a sense in which he must condemn it in order to save it. He condemns everything that we naturally think about God, power, goodness, justice, and the eternal fitness of things. I say 'that we *naturally* think.' There is a natural way of looking at

77

these things, a way congenial to our nature, and we naturally assume that our natural way of thinking is the right way. If we cannot trust our own nature what can we trust? But, answers Christianity, the real question is about just this: our nature. We think it very healthy and sound, a most safe guide and a most sure defense. Christ takes for granted that this nature of ours is corrupt at the root of its being, and this is what he must make all over before we can see God as he is.

Chesterton remarks that the Sermon on the Mount is not a beautiful discourse that our sad but sane planet cannot reasonably accept; rather it is sanity preached to a planet of lunatics. This is the Christian view, and he who holds it must part company with all good, sensible, reasonable people who think 'naturally' about God and man. As Christians we know that our nature is warped and our world crazy.

In an interesting psychological study of biblical faith, Dr. C. J. Jung suggests: 'One should make clear to oneself what it means when God becomes man. It means nothing less than a world-shattering transformation of God.'[1] His remark would be entirely acceptable to Christians if emended to read—'a world-shattering transformation of the *idea* of God.' God does not change when he becomes man; but they who receive Christ undergo a world-shaking transformation of their whole view of God

1. Jung, C. J., *Answer to Job*, London, 1954, p. 63. By permission of Routledge and Kegan Paul, publishers.

and man and all things temporal and eternal. We see Christ and we exclaim in astonishment: 'So this is God! This is ultimate reality! This is power—wisdom—justice—goodness—love! This is life as God means it to be!' And as this transformation takes hold of us it begins to transform ourselves. Then, and only then, do we begin to see how this Gospel of a God who loves us to his own death makes *real* sense, while all else that passes for practical good sense about God is nonsense. How can God give himself away and still keep himself? This sounds like a silly question calling for a silly answer, *until you do some loving after Christ's fashion yourself*. Then you learn the incredible truth that you do keep yourself by giving yourself away, you do find your life by losing it. Christ enriches himself in his incarnation by impoverishing himself for our sake. This is the mystery of true love, divine love, which the world can never know until it sees it demonstrated in Christ. And it is not enough to see it and to believe it. We know it only as we feebly strive to imitate Christ in his loving.

Have in yourselves this mind which is also in Christ Jesus. We are not to be mere adoring spectators of this revolutionary revealed glory of God. We are to have this same mind in us, the mind we see in the God who lives by loving us to his death. There is grave spiritual peril in becoming so enamored of the mind of Christ as we see it in *him* that we cannot move on to our main business as his disciples—the cultivation of that mind in ourselves. In one of Thackeray's letters we find a severe stricture upon

Thomas à Kempis' devotional classic *The Imitation of Christ*. Says Thackeray: 'The scheme of that book carried out would make the world the most wretched, useless, dreary, doting place of sojourn—where would be no manhood, no love, no tender ties of mother and child, no use of intellect, no trade or science, a set of selfish beings crawling about avoiding one another and howling a perpetual *miserere*.' It is a harsh verdict, but there is truth in it in so far as Thomas à Kempis neglects to emphasize that the Crucified is to be not only loved and worshiped but actively imitated in his loving. Too much traditional Christian piety has been directed to the Cross rather than to the Crucified. The Cross of Christ is to be not only seen but shared; and, when it is shared, the joy of the Cross becomes not an idle word but a realized victorious fact.

The mind of Christ in us: it means loving as he loves, hence seeing as he sees; and it must involve suffering as he suffers. There is no Christian claim that love in action always comes out with a happy ending in this world. Love that is at all like Christ's is met with contradiction, with some kind and degree of crucifixion. The Christian claim is that there is joy even in this sadness, victory even in this defeat, life even in this death; and that the joy, victory, and life are those of the Most High God himself. Of such is the kingdom of heaven.

Chapter Thirteen

OBEDIENCE AND FREEDOM

11:12-13.

So then, my beloved, as you were always obedient when I was with you, be even more so in my absence and work out your own salvation with fear and trembling. It is God working in you who causes you both to want, and to work for, his approval.

It was easier for them to be obedient to the mind of Christ when Paul was with them. They had before them his powerful example, his counsel and his faith to draw upon at firsthand. Now, in his absence, they must continue their difficult obedience without having him to lean on for support.

Work out your own salvation. Emphatically it does not mean 'save yourselves by your own effort.' This text is often flagrantly misused by modern disciples of the heretic Pelagius, who taught that it is up to us to save ourselves from our sins. The salvation comes from God; it is God's gift and God's accomplishment in us. Our *working it out* is our acceptance of the gift and our unremitting effort to co-operate with God's grace by giving over our wills to God as he works in us. *With fear and trembling*:

not in anxiety and doubt about God, but about our own selves. When we realize how easily we can block and frustrate God's work in us by our stubbornly resisting his grace we must fear and tremble for the possible consequences. Our fear and trembling concerns our awful responsibility.

It is God working in you who causes you both to want, and to work for, his approval. Paul is repeating the great truth he has earlier mentioned in 1:6. He is not unsaying what he has just said about working out our own salvation. He is directing our minds away from our own frailty, about which we must fear and tremble, to our real hope and security: God working in us, giving us both the desire to please him and the grace and power to do it.

This little admonition to obedience and trust in God rather than in ourselves is an abrupt let-down after the sublime flight of the kenosis hymn. Paul's transitions are often like this. His speaking must have been like his writing, full of startling changes of pace. He is never the cool systematic thinker, moving with majestic orderliness from point to point in a fine progression of cumulative cogency. Yet there is a connection—indicated by the *So then* with which he opens this passage—between what he has just said and what he is now saying. Because Christ has demonstrated his power and love for us so tremendously in his self-emptying for our sake, therefore we can continue our patient obedience to him in the assurance that he can and will save us. We have a Saviour who can do what we have seen him do in his passion and death, his resurrection and ascension; now let us get on with the proper business of our lives, which is to make our lives our response to his love, our thank-offering to him.

Why then need there be any *fear and trembling* in the Christian's heart? There is only too good cause for it. With this mighty God to trust in, we are none the less under constant temptation to spurn that fortress and to trust in our own selves. Explain it how you will, the fact is that we are far from being fully emancipated from the old man Adam in us, who is dying but not dead. We relapse into our pre-Christian state, in which every man tries to go it alone on his quest of goodness. There is nothing peculiarly Christian about wanting to be good. Every rational person wants to be good. The difference between the Christian and the non-Christian seekers of goodness is seen, not so much in their goals as in their ways of seeking and striving for goodness. The Christian knows that he is not a self-made man but a derivative man. He seeks goodness by giving himself over wholly to the grace of God in Jesus Christ, putting his sole trust in that. The natural man does it by rolling up his sleeves, taking his life in hand, and making (or trying to make) this 'good' thing even better. He is trusting in himself; and it seems manly, sensible, courageous, and 'natural' even to the Christian, who must fear and tremble lest he succumb to this solicitation of the devil. St. Basil, the great Cappadocian bishop of the fourth century, was a very holy man at the time he wrote to a friend: 'I hesitate to write what I myself do in this solitude, night and day, seeing that, although I have left the distractions of the city, which are to me the occasion of innumerable evils, I have not yet succeeded in forsaking myself.' The grim fight was still on for him, the struggle to transfer his trust from self to God.

What then can the Christian do? He can only continue to fight this battle within himself until the Lord gives him the final victory. He fights it by daily, constantly, renewing his self-oblation to his Lord with all his heart and will, in the spirit of Ignatius Loyola's prayer: 'Take, O Lord, and receive all my liberty, my memory, my understanding, and all my will, all I have and possess: you have given it to me; to you, O Lord, I return it; all is yours; dispose of it entirely according to your will. Give me your love and grace, because that is enough for me.'

Paul reminds the Philippians that they must continue in their obedience to the Lord while Paul is no longer there with them. This is going to be harder. It always is, under such circumstances. Whom had they been obeying while Paul was with them—Paul, or Christ? The truth must be admitted, that Paul was a very firm-handed pastor whose critics thought him very high-handed. Clerical autocracy is always a temptation in church life, not only to priest and prelate but to the laity. To have a pastor whom one can simply obey without argument solves a lot of problems for the bewildered soul. But if we read thoughtfully the evidences concerning Paul's pastoral dealings with people we see what his real object was. It was to make them obedient to the Lord rather than to himself. They had been leaning on him at Philippi, perhaps too much, when he was with them. Now they must lean upon the Lord who cannot be taken from them. The right business of the Christian pastor is to lead his people into a complete dependence upon the Lord. He must not let himself become the Lord's proxy or substitute. Yet if he is to do this he must have their dependence on himself, of a sort, in a degree; and the right way of securing this is to be the kind of man Paul is—one who himself practices that total self-commitment to obedience to Christ which he preaches to them.

But is not obedience, even obedience to the Lord, a slavish virtue? Where is this 'freedom in Christ' we hear so much about, if we must *obey* him? Inevitably the modern democratic mind asks the question, and not without reason. We learn from history that a passion for obedience in the masses is just what would-be tyrants and enslavers want.

> *Power, like a desolating pestilence,*
> *Pollutes whate'er it touches; and obedience,*
> *Bane of all genius, virtue, freedom, truth,*
> *Makes slaves of men, and of the human frame*
> *A mechanized automaton.*
>
> (SHELLEY, *Queen Mab*. III.)

The Christian need not quarrel with Shelley's rebel yell against obedience to tyrants. There is peril even in obedience to the Church, if we understand it as Loyola defines it in the Constitution of the Jesuits (Part 6, chapter 1, section 1): 'We must, if anything appears to our eyes white, which the Church declares to be black, also declare it to be black.' Our obedience is to be only to the Lord; yet we can give it to him only as we hear his commands through his Church. When Christ's minister speaks to us the word of the Lord, and we obey it, we are obeying Christ. And we may lay this down as a safe rule of action: if any Christian sincerely wants to hear the Lord's word that he may obey it, he will hear it.

We dare not obey any man purely passively and unthinkingly, lest we become 'a mechanized automaton.' But our obedience to Jesus Christ is not liable to this error. For one thing, we can trust him as we can trust no mortal man. What does he seek except our own good? But there is an even more compelling and unique consideration: we belong to him. We are his, to do with as he wills. No creature can belong, *de jure*, to another creature. No man can be the possession or tool of another man without violating the very principle of his own existence as a created being. Man belongs only to him who creates him and gives him being, and Christ is 'he by whom all things were made.'

Obedience to Christ is the fulfillment of man. This is Paul's gospel, and he had found it wonderfully true for himself. He gloried in being a slave of Jesus Christ because it gave him a freedom undreamed of before: the freedom to fulfill his own true self. The violin is a poor thing when it is used as a sledge-hammer, because obviously he who uses it thus does not know how to use it. In the hands of its true master the violin comes into its own, by its own obedience to its owner's loving and skillful artistry. Man likewise is a poor thing when owned and used by another man, or by himself. He comes into his own when he who truly owns him takes him in hand; and man makes this possible by his obedience to Jesus Christ, who comes to put us into God's hands where we eternally belong and where alone we can be what we are made to be.

Chapter Fourteen

'IN RECTITUDE, BEAUTY'

11:14-18.

Do everything without grumbling and argument, so that you may be free from fault, straightforward, unspoiled children of God living among an unenlightened and twisted people. Among such you appear as bright stars in the world, holding out to them the word of life. This will be my boast in the day of Christ, the proof that I did not run and work in vain. And if my life is poured out as a libation upon the sacrifice and service of your faith, I am glad, and I rejoice with you all. For this same reason, be glad and rejoice with me.

Perhaps Paul remembers the valedictory of Moses, who had to leave this world with his people in a most unsatisfactory spiritual condition: 'They have corrupted themselves, their spot is not the spot of his children: they are a perverse and crooked generation' (Deut. 32:5). His Philippians are much better than that, but not so good that they cannot fall into the easy and nasty habit of doing things with *grumbling and argument*. Remarkably good people can yet make their goodness remarkably unattractive by the ungraciousness of their ways.

88

They are *living among an unenlightened and twisted people,* among whom they *appear as bright stars, holding out to them the word of life*: that is, the Gospel as the light of the world.

This will be my boast in the day of Christ, the proof that I did not run and work in vain. Their way of living the Christian life will draw others to the source of their light. His 'running' is an athletic metaphor. The contestants in the games run for a prize. The prize for which he has been striving is the completion of his task of preparing Christ's people for their work of effectively witnessing to their Lord in the world. The divine judge will bestow the prizes *in the day of Christ.*

And if my life is poured out as a libation upon the sacrifice and service of your faith, I am glad and I rejoice with you all. The metaphor is built upon sacrificial ritual. Their faith is their sacrifice and their service of God. They have offered it; and if Paul is called upon to pour out his blood this will be the libation which completes the sacrifice. *I am glad* to do this, and *I rejoice with you all* in this triumphant conclusion of their common sacrifice. They are not to be sad if they hear that Paul has died: rather, *be glad and rejoice with me.* (In my translation I have turned Paul's indicative mood into the imperative, because he is in fact exhorting them to rejoice with him in the event of his death.)

'The spirit of man is the candle of the Lord.' (Provs. 20:27.) When the spirit of man is alight with the flame of God's Spirit, man is indeed a bright star in the world, holding out to others the word of life. In Plato's *Symposium,* Alcibiades is quoted as saying that Socrates is like one of those ugly Silenus-figures which you open to find golden images of the gods gleaming at you from inside. The gaiety of Socrates, his charm and courtesy, were the outward and visible means by which earnest seekers of truth were drawn to the wisdom he preached. There must be this same congruity, in the Christian's life, between his inner loyalty to the light of the world and the outward expression of it on that side of his life which other people see and touch. A Scotsman once testified, 'I am a Christian because the Reverend Doctor Marcus Dods is a Christian. Talk about the evidences of Christianity, Dods is it.'

Paul's admonition to do all things *without grumbling and argument* speaks to every Christian's condition. We shall be totally useless to our Lord as his agents, his walking advertisements, if people see us as grumbling, grudging, contentious souls, going through the Christian motions simply because it is our duty and we must do it.

We cannot exaggerate the value of courtesy and graciousness as a part of our Christian duty. Coventry Patmore said that courtesy is the only virtue that will be practiced in heaven. Can it be so? Won't we need courage? No, for there is nothing to fear in heaven. Sympathy? But there is no pain in heaven to elicit our sympathy. Temperance? In heaven we shall have passed beyond the need for self-control. Hope? The object of our hope will be fully attained. But courtesy, the outward expression of charity, will be there in full flower.

The judicious Hooker lays it down in his *Ecclesiastical Polity* that 'goodness in actions is like unto straightness; wherefore that which is done well we term *right*. For as the straight is what is most acceptable to him that travelleth, because by it he cometh soonest to his journey's end; so in action, that which doth lie the evenest between us and the end we desire most needs to be the fittest for our use. Besides which fitness for use, there is also in rectitude, beauty; as contrariwise in obliquity, deformity. And that which is good in the actions of men, doth not only delight as profitable, but as amiable also. In which consideration the Grecians most divinely have given to the active perfection of men a name expressing both beauty and goodness, because goodness in ordinary speech is for the most part applied only to that which is beneficial. But we in the name of goodness do here imply both.'

Christian goodness is both beneficial and amiable, else it is not the real thing. 'In rectitude, beauty!' When our living both shows to others what they ought to be and makes them want to be it we *appear as bright stars in the world, holding out* to others *the word of life*. Marcus Dods was one man's evidence of Christianity, and he made the man want what Dods had. Ultimately, this is the only kind of Christian evangelism that ever wins anybody.

A little girl was once overheard praying: 'Dear Lord, make all bad people good, and all good people nice.' She had the Christian idea.

In this brief passage Paul deals with two different matters. The first we have considered: the matter of living our Christian life winsomely and making our goodness attractive. The second is the matter of his possible martyrdom.

If he dies a martyr, it will be because he has worked to make his people what they are, and he has succeeded in making them Christians who give to God *the sacrifice and service of their faith*. This has been accomplished; if he must now die, he can depart in peace knowing that his work is done. Then, *in the day of Christ*, when the Lord asks him what he has done on earth, he can point to them as his *boast*. Hence he has reason to be glad, and he wants them to be glad if the word comes to them that he has been put to death.

The man with a work to do for God has only one thing to fear about death: that it may cut him off with his work not done. When his work is done, if he dies for having done it his blood is the libation of love and devotion which gives his work the grand finishing touch and makes it a perfect offering. He who has sown in tears now reaps in joy.

Chapter Fifteen

FRIENDSHIP IN CHRIST

11:19-30.

I hope in the Lord Jesus to send Timothy to you soon, so that I may be cheered by hearing about your affairs. I have no one else of congenial mind who will honestly put your welfare first. All the others serve their own interests rather than the interests of Jesus Christ. But you know his worth, and how he worked with me as a child with his father in the service of the Gospel. Therefore I hope to send him as soon as I see how my own situation develops; but I trust in the Lord that I will soon be coming to you myself. Even so, I have decided that I must send to you Epaphroditus, my brother and co-worker and fellow soldier, and your messenger and minister to my need. For he has been longing for all of you, and distressed because you heard that he was ill. He was, in fact, sick nearly to death, but God had mercy on him — and on me, so that I should not suffer grief piled upon grief. So I sent him all the sooner, that you may have the pleasure of seeing him again and I may be less anxious. Receive him in the Lord most joyfully, and hold such men in honor, for he came near to death for the word of Christ, risking his life in carrying out your ministry to me in my need.

I hope in the Lord Jesus means here 'if the Lord Jesus grants my wish.' Timothy is well known to them as Paul's assistant on previous visits (Acts 16:1f. and I Cor.

93

16:20). Paul is worried about some things in Philippi, and hopes to be *cheered by hearing about your affairs* when Timothy returns to him.

We are curious about *all the others* who put their own welfare ahead of Christ's cause. They must be Christians who visit Paul in his cell and whom he cannot trust with the mission to Philippi. If they are Roman Christians, Paul may mean by his charge that they put their own interests ahead of the interests of Jesus Christ, or simply that they are narrowly parochial in their concern, caring little for the welfare of Christians beyond their own parish, in Philippi or elsewhere.

I have decided that I must send to you Epaphroditus. This he has already done. Timothy will come later. Epaphroditus had brought money to Paul from the Philippians (4:8). Like Timothy, he is a true *brother and co-worker and fellow soldier,* whose loyalty has been a mighty comfort to Paul. He has been desperately sick and homesick, and now seems to be the time to send him back to Philippi. They will be delighted to see him again, and Paul will be *less anxious,* presumably because Epaphroditus' life is in constant danger while he is in Rome and Paul does not want to be responsible for his needless exposure to peril.

⌖

Timothy and Epaphroditus were Paul's friends in the Lord. Timothy is a friend Paul can trust because he is

94

not one of those who *serve their own interests rather than the interests of Jesus Christ*. A friend who is amiable, but not trustworthy, is not a complete friend; and what makes Timothy worthy of Paul's trust is his self-denying devotion to Jesus Christ. Epaphroditus has proved himself trustworthy for the same reason, so this primary principle of friendship is found in them both.

They manifest their friendship by sharing Paul's pain and danger. 'A friend loveth at all times, and a brother is born for adversity.' (Provs. 17:17.)

We tend to think that real friendship is a much commoner thing than it is. Romain Rolland is nearer the truth, in this reflection in *Jean Christophe*: 'The world's misery lies in this, that a man hardly ever has a companion. Women perhaps, and chance friendships. We are reckless in our use of the lovely word, friend. In reality we hardly have a single friend all through our lives. Rare, very rare, are those men who have real friends. But the happiness of it is so great that it is impossible to live when they are gone. The friend filled the life of his friend, unbeknown to him, unmarked. The friend goes: and life is empty. Not only the beloved is lost, but every reason for loving, every reason for having loved. Why had he lived? Why had either lived?'

Paul would probably agree with the first part of Rolland's statement and disagree with the second part. True, those men who have real friends are very rare; but the Christian can never say that life is worthless and meaningless when the friend is gone. He still has his perfect and changeless friend, the divine companion. He still has also all his friends in Christ, whether they be present with him in the flesh or absent, the communion of saints in heaven and earth. The departure of a friend is not the sad end of a beautiful chapter for the Christian. Rolland's reflection is heavy with the sadness of all purely human and earthly love. In Christ, one never loses a friend.

There are various degrees and kinds of friendship. On the lowest level is the kind that consists of mere 'suiting one another.' This friendship is well described in a typical occurrence of it in Trollope's *Framley Parsonage*: 'Mrs. Harold Smith had spoken no more than the truth in saying that she and Miss Dunstable suited one another. And she had not improperly described their friendship. They were not prepared to die, one for the sake of the other. They had said nothing to each other of mutual love and affection. They never kissed, or cried, or made speeches, when they met or when they parted. There was no great benefit for which either had to be grateful to the other; no terrible injury which either had forgiven. But they suited each other; and this, I take it, is the secret of most of our pleasantest intercourse in the world.'

On a higher level stands the friendship which brings to one in trouble a wonderful sense that life is, after all, worth living. Shakespeare gives it a matchless description:

When in disgrace with fortune and men's eyes
I all alone beweep my outcast state,
And trouble deaf heaven with my bootless cries,
And look upon myself and curse my fate

Wishing me like to one more rich in hope,
Featured like him, like him with friends possessed,
Desiring this man's art, and that man's scope,
With what I most enjoy contented least;

Yet in these thoughts myself almost despising,
Haply I think on thee—and then my state,
Like to the lark at break of day arising
From sullen earth, sings hymns at heaven's gate;

For thy sweet love remembered, such wealth brings
That then I scorn to change my state with kings.

The friend who can do this for you must be more than merely charming and agreeable. He must have something of that self-giving loyalty which Timothy and Epaphroditus showed toward Paul; his friendship must cost him something. We may be diverted from our troubles by the jolly but shallow friend; we cannot be deeply cheered and sustained by him.

On the highest level of friendship is that which knit together Paul and Timothy and Epaphroditus in a holy, sanctifying, and deathless bond: friendship *in Christ*. They belong to one another absolutely and eternally because they belong to Christ. Such friendship brings the strength and joy that is so rich in my Japanese friend and his family mentioned earlier. The union of men with God,

says Aquinas, is the union of men with one another. Its
reality is expressed in the hymn:

> *Blest be the tie that binds*
> *Our hearts in Jesus' love;*
> *The fellowship of kindred minds*
> *Is like to that above.*
>
> *Before our Father's throne*
> *We pour united prayers,*
> *Our fears, our hopes, our aims are one,*
> *Our comforts and our cares.*
>
> *We share our mutual woes*
> *Our mutual burdens bear,*
> *And often for each other flows*
> *The sympathizing tear.*
>
> *When we at death must part,*
> *Not like the world's our pain;*
> *But one in Christ, and one in heart,*
> *We part to meet again.*
>
> (JOHN FAWCETT, 1782, *alt.*)

This is what friendship in Christ is, means, and does; and
the experience of it is heaven begun.

Chapter Sixteen

THE TRUE CIRCUMCISION

III:1-7.

Finally, my brothers, rejoice in the Lord. To write these things to you is not irksome to me, and it is prudent for your sake. Beware of the dogs, beware of the evil-doers, beware of the party of the circumcision. For we are the truly circumcised, we who worship God in Spirit and who make our boast, not in a privileged human status, but in Christ Jesus. I happen to have some basis for 'trusting' in that! If anybody else can rely on this, I can make a better claim: circumcised on the eighth day, of the people of Israel, of the tribe of Benjamin, a Hebrew of Hebrews, a Pharisee concerning the Law, a zealous persecutor of the Church, a perfect practitioner of that righteousness of the Law. But whatever I then considered a profit to me I now consider loss for Christ's sake.

Here is the great problem passage. Verses 1b-19, beginning with *To write these things*, contain a polemical diatribe against the *dogs* and *evil-workers*. There is no good reason to doubt that it was written by Paul, but there are weighty reasons for doubting that he wrote it at the time of writing the Letter as a whole. Most probably he wrote it at an earlier date, when the work of the Judaizers was a serious threat to the church in Philippi. According to this theory the earlier writing was saved, and later was attached to the Letter as we have it now.

The passage does not fit where it now stands; the change in both tone and topic is too drastic. Yet we cannot rule out as impossible the theory of a single writing. It is conceivable that Paul had written the Letter through chapter two and was just beginning the closing section with something like 'Rejoice in the Lord (3:1), for our citizenship is in heaven' (3:20) when a messenger interrupted him with the news that the Judaizers were now raising havoc in Philippi. Then in anger and anxiety he launched into this subject immediately, with no regard to the literary unity of his letter. Paul is given to these quick changes of thought and mood. But that this is the explanation here is almost too much to believe. The most plausible theory is that verses 1b—19 are interpolated from an earlier letter by Paul. If we omit this section and connect 1a with 20ff. we get a very plausible order: *Finally, my brothers, rejoice in the Lord. For our citizenship is established in heaven, whence we await a Saviour, the Lord Jesus Christ.*

In any case, we are dealing with an unquestionably authentic writing of Paul.

To write these things to you is not irksome to me, and it is prudent for your sake. He means the warning about to follow, which he has written to them perhaps many times before. He does not mind repeating it, since the matter is so important and the warning so necessary for their sake.

Beware of the dogs, beware of the evil-doers, be-

ware of the party of the circumcision. Who are the *dogs*? They can hardly be the insincere and partisan preachers dealt with in 1:15f., for Paul questions only the motivation of their preaching, not their doctrine itself. The objects of this present denunciation are Jews: either Jews who are not Christians at all, or Judaizing Christians who think that everybody must become a Jew to become a Christian. This second possibility seems the stronger. The fact that the Judaizers were Christians, and very zealous ones, would make them the more dangerously persuasive to their Gentile brethren.

The epithets Paul bestows upon them are discourteous, to say the least. But each of them has a definite point of meaning; this is not simply angry and indiscriminate name-calling. *Dogs* are despised in the East because they eat garbage. If Christians are now God's children, why should they live on 'the garbage of carnal ordinances' (Lightfoot) when God calls them to the feast of his love? They are *evil-doers* in that they work an evil debasement of Christianity. *The party of the circumcision* is a free translation; Paul's Greek word literally means the mutilation of the flesh. The Judaizers believed that the ritual act of mutilating the flesh in circumcision brought men into privileged status with God.

For we are the truly circumcised, we who worship God in Spirit and who make our boast, not in a privileged human status, but in Christ Jesus. Paul will not concede that the Judaizers, for all their talk about the saving power of circumcision, are *truly circumcised* at all. The proper meaning of circumcision, as an outward and visible act, is that it signifies the inward and spiritual covenant between God and the people he has chosen. It is the thing signified that matters. The Christian enters into this spiritual covenant with God *in Christ Jesus,* and the outward sign of admission to it that the Lord has provided is not circumcision but baptism. To suggest then that a Christian must be not only baptized but circumcised is to revise the Lord's own appointments.

We who worship God in Spirit. The text has no definite article before *Spirit;* the Holy Spirit is clearly meant. True worship is offered when the Holy Spirit moves the worshiper to offer it, and not by the smug consideration that because he has been circumcised he has a *privileged human status* with God as one of God's elect. We who *make our boast in Christ Jesus* are not boasting of our own status, or merits, or achievements; our only boast is Christ himself, who has chosen us not because of our merits but out of the unfathomable depths of his love.

But it is easy for people who happen to lack *privileged human status* to throw stones at those who have it. When the poor man rails against the rich, or the ignoramus against whom he regards as the 'bookful blockhead, ignorantly read, with loads of learned lumber in his head,' it may be sour grapes. Paul is saying that such a motive cannot be his. *As for privileged human status, I happen to have some basis for 'trusting' in that!* He has everything the Judaizer could crave: birth of the revered tribe of Benjamin; circumcision; the best of training in the Law, and so eminent a reputation for living up to this meticulous legal righteousness that any Pharisee might envy him. He once thought that all this was of great profit to him. Now that he has Christ he knows how valueless it all was.

◅━

It is an old, old story in religion: the apparently insatiable desire of the God-hungry soul to work out a system of 'works-righteousness.' The conflict between Paul and the contemporary Judaizers is only one battle in a universal and unending conflict. These Judaizers wanted two things. They wanted a way of dealing with God which would guarantee their salvation—something they could *do* that would make it all easy and safe. Circumcision, with the adoption of the onerous Mosaic Law, might seem a hard enough course for frail human flesh, but once that course was taken one had only to stick to it—to do this and to abstain from doing that—and God would have to give you what you earned. This was one thing they wanted.

The other thing they wanted goes right along with the first: *privileged human status*. They wanted a religion which would make them superior to other men, so that they could be envied, admired, looked up to. We are indebted to Reinhold Niebuhr in our day for showing us how pride gets into our religion, in a way both subtle and devastating, so that while we say or think we are pleasing God we are in reality pleasing our vain selves with the thought of how much better are we than other men. We can be proud even of our humility! This truth is illustrated by the story of the Carthusian monk who was explaining to a stranger the ethos of his order. Said he: 'We're not in a class with the Jesuits in learning. The Franciscans excel us in good works. The Dominicans are much better preachers than we are. But when it comes to humility, we're tops!'

No religious body or individual is free from this temptation. We want to be able to boast in ourselves rather than in the Lord Jesus Christ. We want a religion that is both *safe* and *flattering*.

A safe religion is one in which we are sure of getting what we want from God, regardless of whether it is what God wants for us: a religion that 'works,' that 'gets results.' *Do ut des*: 'I give in order that thou mayst give.' 'I am circumcised so that You will have to include me among Your elect; I say my prayers so that You will have to cure my sick child; I go to church so that You will have to prosper my business; I meditate upon Your power and love so that You will have to give me peace of mind and freedom from tension.' Our tactics may be very crude or very refined, very childish or very sophisticated; but so long as we concentrate upon getting what we want from God we are spiritually akin to the Judaizers.

And we want a *flattering* religion—a church we can be proud to belong to! It is hard to criticize this motive without seeming to criticize a very good and reasonable thing. If a Christian communion exhibits a glorious history of saints and heroes of Christ, if it teaches sound doctrine, if it has a liturgy richly expressive of the beauty of holiness, are these not good and right reasons for belonging to it? Certainly they are. And yet, how easily such proper pride becomes an excuse for complacency, arrogance, and thanking God that we are not as other men are!

The right business of the Church is to glorify Christ and not itself. His—not the Church's—is the kingdom, the power, and the glory. This is what the Church and churchmen must keep foremost in mind at all times. Emil Brunner submits this sobering *caveat*:

'Religion expresses not only the inner reality of the holy, but at the same time always its externalization. It localizes the holy, making it administrable, manipulable. It makes man a claimful partner in the affairs of God, instigating him to demand what can only be a free gift of grace. Thus it kills the idea of the servant of God who is free from the law and from the self-righteous attitude of the *homo religiosus* by freely imparted divine love. Hence the Kingdom of God represents the overcoming of religion just as much as its consummation. For it is the Kingdom of Him who was execrated and executed as a criminal offender against religion by religious men, not by any religious men, but by the best of religious men. It is said of the City of God: "I saw no temple therein." '[1]

1. Brunner, Emil, *Eternal Hope*, Philadelphia, 1954, p. 165. By permission of The Westminster Press, publishers.

Paul has gone through the stage of being a 'claimful partner in the affairs of God,' and now, looking back on it all, he says that it was all *loss for Christ's sake*. It was all spiritual bankruptcy, however rich he thought it was at the time: belonging to the right church, being admired for his zeal in practicing what he believed in and in persecuting what he disbelieved in, being in a position (as he thought at the time) to manipulate God. Now he has a much harder religion, in a sense; certainly a humiliating one. He has nothing to boast of on his own behalf. The moment he is tempted to congratulate himself on being a pretty good Christian he recalls the man Christ Jesus, and he realizes what a pitiable excuse for a Christian he is. He must recognize now that whatever goodness he may have comes not by his own achievement but solely by the gracious gift of God. But now he is happy and at peace as he could never have dreamed of being before. The loss of all the old ridiculous grounds for boasting in himself has brought to him the inestimable and glorious gain of being in Christ; and in the passage that now follows he tries to tell us why this is, and what it is.

Chapter Seventeen

WHAT IT IS TO BE SAVED

III:8-11.

*Indeed, I count everything to be worthless compared
to the incomparable treasure of knowing Christ Jesus my Lord,
for whom I have given up everything. I count it all as refuse
in order to gain Christ and to be found in him having, not a
righteousness of my own coming from the Law, but that
righteousness which comes through faith in Christ—the righteousness given by God and resting on a man's faith. This is
the righteousness of knowing him, the power of his resurrection and the fellowship of his sufferings, of being conformed
to his dying in such a way that I may possibly attain to the
resurrection from the dead.*

This confession comes out of a passion of gratitude to Christ for having raised Paul to a totally new life.
Everything he associates with his pre-Christian experience, its richest rewards and deepest satisfactions, now
seem so paltry compared to what Christ has given him that
he can only *count it all as refuse,* as worthless, cast-off
rubbish.

It is no vain boast or plaintive self-pity when he
says *I have given up everything.* He now realizes that it was
not worth keeping anyway.

I count it all as refuse in order to gain Christ and to be found in him. The tense and the mood suggest his continuing renunciation and devaluation of the things he once considered of highest worth. It is only as the Christian is constantly renouncing the things that come between him and his Lord that he can keep them out of his life and thus enjoy *the incomparable treasure of knowing Christ.* This *knowing Christ* is not mere intellectual knowledge, but a most intimate personal relationship of loving self-commitment to Christ as *my Lord.* The knowledge of Christ is vital union with him, living in him.

In the distinction between *a righteousness of my own coming from the Law* and *that righteousness which comes through faith in Christ* Paul touches upon the great theme of his Letter to the Romans, where it should be studied in its full exposition. Here we may state the distinction between the two kinds of righteousness in terms of the last judgment as Paul foresees it. His one hope is that he will be found faithful at the last in his answer to Christ's call to trust in him. If he were still living by the Law's righteousness his hope would be very different. It would be that the divine judge would look over his record of good works and see that he had done well. This would be a judgment according to his self-achieved merits. But Paul is now convinced that Christ the judge will have another question to ask: 'Have you trusted in me, rather than in your own self?'

This faith-righteousness, as distinct from works-righteousness, is *the righteousness given by God* (rather than the righteousness achieved by man) *and resting on a man's faith. This is the righteousness of knowing him, the power of his resurrection and the fellowship of his sufferings, of being conformed to his dying in such a way that I may possibly attain to the resurrection from the dead.* To know Christ, in this sense of trusting him completely and loving and serving him devotedly, is the only righteousness a Christian can have, and it is *given by God.* Knowing Christ is identification with Christ in one's own life in such a way that one experiences the Life of Christ in himself. Paul mentions *the power of his resurrection* before *the fellowship of his sufferings* because this is the right order in the Christian life: we first receive the resurrection power by entering into living union with the risen Lord, then we experience his cross as we take up the tasks he gives us to do.

In the words *being conformed to his dying in such a way that I may possibly attain to the resurrection from the dead* Paul touches upon his concept of dying and rising with Christ, which is more fully presented in Romans 6. He knows that he has died to his old self and has been raised to a new being. Yet this dying and raising is still in process, and the final issue is still undecided. What remains must be a matter of hope— that he may attain to the final and eternal resurrection victory. He is hopeful rather than certain about this, not because he has any doubt of the Lord's will and power to give him the final victory, but because he dares not take his own perseverance in the faith for granted.

Elsewhere (I Cor. 9:27) he acknowledges with startling candor the possibility that he, having preached to others, might himself be found a castaway at last: not through Christ's failure but his own.

Christians who claim to have 'the assurance of final salvation' as a result of having been 'saved' are claiming more for themselves than Paul dared to claim for himself.

'Salvation' is one of the key words of Christianity; but because so many half-truths and total falsehoods have become associated with it we wish we could find a good English synonym for it, so that we could use the word without having to distinguish its true meaning from its familiar perversions and parodies. When William Tyndale translated the New Testament into the English of his day (1525-26) he rendered Christ's words about Zacchaeus as 'This day is health come to this house' (St. Luke 19:9). The Authorized Version reads 'salvation' where Tyndale has 'health.' By 'health' Tyndale meant wholeness, soundness, completeness of life, and this is essentially what Christ's salvation is.

Paul tells us that he never knew what it is to live—to be hale, whole, until Christ captured him and made him his own.

The first thing to realize about the Christian salvation is that it is God's doing and free gift, not man's own achievement. As the Christian philosopher A. E. Taylor puts it: 'The initiative in the process of "assimilation to God" must come from the side of the eternal; it must be God who first comes to meet us, and who, all through the moral life itself, "works in us," in a sense that is more than metaphorical. Our moral endeavors must be genuinely ours, but they must be responses to intimate actual contacts in which a real God moves outward to meet His creatures, and by the contact at once sustains and inspires the appropriate response on the creature's part.'[1]

The only Christian righteousness is a loving, grateful response to the divine call that comes to us through Jesus Christ. We are forgiven; we are accepted as his children; he asks only that we love him and obey him. He even gives us the will to respond to his call. Once we have responded, if we reflect upon 'what has happened to us,' we see, as Paul saw, that this 'righteousness' of ours is not really ours but God's. We have nothing at all that we have not received. And henceforth, in our passion of gratitude to Christ for all that he gives us, we have (if we are truly in the state of grace) but one desire: to be perfectly conformed, fully subjected, to Christ himself. The saved Christian is he who belongs, body and soul, to his Lord, so that he shares not only Christ's resurrection but his sufferings. We are saved as we are carried up into the life of Christ in both its humiliation and sufferings and its resur-

1. Taylor, A. E., *The Faith of a Moralist*, London, 1930, Series 1, p. 223. By permission of The Macmillan Company, and St Martin's Press.

rection and victory; and we are carried up into this life as we hear God's great invitation, spoken to us by Christ, and respond to it.

One sure sign of the soul's true salvation is its sorrow for sin: its own sin and the sin of the world. Here is the mystery of *the fellowship of his sufferings*. Francis of Assisi was a joyful saint, but he suffered agonies of contrition for the sin of the world. John Woolman, the Quaker saint of 18th-century America, enjoyed a rare, rich communion with God, but the wretchedness of the slaves was his own wretchedness. Since Christ suffers in all who suffer, the true saint feels acutely as his own the pains and woes of the least of his brethren. We are saved, not only by the cross of Christ, but into it. To be *conformed to his dying* is to experience Christ's suffering.

Paul desired to do this *in such a way that I may possibly attain to the resurrection from the dead*. As we noted in our exegesis, Paul cannot indulge the luxury that some Christians feel entitled to, of saying 'Christ has saved me and I am his forever'—as though it were a fixed, settled, and final thing. Too much popular religious revivalism concentrates, only too successfully, upon creating this illusion of 'being saved for keeps' in those whom it converts. There is no New Testament warrant for any assurance of final salvation for anybody. For the soul retains its power to resist and reject God's grace to the end, and that stark fact destroys the possibility of any once-for-all settlement of the issue of one's eternal salvation at some given moment in time. The moment of decision for Christ or against him is every moment of life until the end, when our probation is over and our case is unalterably closed by God's final verdict. Such is the New Testament teaching, and such is Paul's conviction about salvation.

But there is an assurance we can possess here and now: the assurance that so long as we go on trusting Christ and entrusting our whole being to him he will go on saving us. He is faithful. The only questionable factor is our own faithfulness, our perseverance to the end.

Chapter Eighteen

THE CHRISTIAN INVESTIGATION OF GOD

III:12-16.

Not that I have received the prize, or am already perfect; but I push on that perhaps I might receive it, since I have been received myself by Christ Jesus. Brethren, I do not consider myself as one who has received, but one thing I do: forgetting what lies behind me and stretching forward to the things ahead I push on toward the goal, toward the prize of the upward calling of God in Christ Jesus. For all of us who are mature Christians, then, let this be our principle; and if any of you are of another mind, God will show this to you. Let us make it our rule to walk by the truth we have already learned.

We may have got the impression from the passage immediately preceding this one that the Christian has nothing to do but trust for his salvation. In a deep sense this is true. But trusting means actual pushing on with the life of obedient service; faith means work. Paul wants to make this very clear, and he wants also to emphasize that he is not setting himself up as a perfect model. He too is on the way, with a long way to go himself, and all that he can claim is that he has found the right way. He is making still another point: his adversaries, the Judaizers, are self-perfectionists. They believe that perfection is humanly achievable and in this life. Paul is worried by the thought that possibly some of his Philippians have been snared by this attractive delusion and think that they have already reached their goal in Christ. No deceit of the devil can be more ruinous to the Christian than this.

Not that I have already received the prize, or am already perfect. A perfect person in Paul's language, is a completed person, fully grown-up in Christ. Paul is far from being this. *But I push on that perhaps I might receive* the prize of perfection. The contingent element of *perhaps I might* is very marked in the Greek (lit. 'I pursue if also I shall receive'). He is not taking for granted his final attainment of the goal. *Since I have been received myself by Christ Jesus* I push on that I might receive it. His profoundest personal experience is that Christ has received, laid hold upon, him. The Lord cannot have done this without a purpose in mind. The Lord's purpose is to set Paul's face *toward the prize of the upward calling of God in Christ Jesus.* This *upward calling of God* raises men from self to God. The calling is to come up higher to share in God's own life. It comes to us by Christ, and to follow him is to answer the call.

For all of us who are mature Christians, then, let this be our principle; and if any of you are of another mind, God will show this to you. We are supplying the word 'Christians,' which is not in the text, to give the full sense. *If any are of another mind, God will show this to you,* provided only that they make it their rule *to walk by the truth we have already learned*. Our knowledge of God's will and ways may be very faulty, but so long as we walk faithfully by the light we have already received from God we shall learn more as we go.

↩

In this passage Paul is saying, 'I don't think for a moment that I have already reached the goal God has set before me. I can say only this for myself: that I turn my back on my past and I face toward my future with God. He has laid hold on me for some reason, and that reason I see in Jesus Christ. He wants me to push on toward conformity to Christ as my eternal prize. This much I see, and this I do. Perhaps some of you don't quite agree that this is our duty and destiny as Christians. I won't argue about that. If you are living up to the truth God has already given you, I am sure that he will show you this truth which grips me, in his good time and way.'

Here is a truly dynamic philosophy of life, whose vital principle is that Christ is *the clue to the meaning of existence*. To know the meaning of our existence is something very different from knowing 'all the answers.' It is to see one clue to life and to follow it with the profound assurance that your clue points you toward your eternal destiny. Thomas Masaryk, one-time president of the Czechoslovakian republic, declared his conviction, after a long life of hard thinking and high statesmanship, that the meaning of all human history is Jesus Christ. He meant by this that whatever in human hope and endeavor is conformed to Christ is headed toward the right goal and has all the power of ultimate reality behind it, while everything that is against Christ is doomed: as doomed as a heavier-than-air object trying to rise by its own weight rather than to fall.

Such is Paul's clue; and a clue, by its very nature, is an article of faith rather than a rule of thumb. When you are following a sound clue, you may grow increasingly convinced that you are on the right track as you go along, but you are still a seeker rather than a finder. Paul urges us to *make it our rule to walk by the truth we have already learned*. Suppose we have learned—by experience as well as teaching—that God is good, that Christ is our true light, that the Holy Spirit unfailingly strengthens our infirmities and makes us sufficient for all trials. Having come thus far in this way, we say 'We don't know everything yet, but we find that the way of Christ is the only way that seems to take us anywhere.' This is to follow Christ as our clue to the meaning of life. It leaves many questions unanswered, such as: 'Why is this way so rough?' 'Why is Christ so clear and compelling to me and not to my wistfully agnostic friend, who is a better man than I am?' 'Why are there so many stumbling-blocks in the Gospel to the rational mind?' 'Why do Christians of equal sincerity and understanding differ so widely in their interpretations of their Master's teachings?' These and many other questions must await their answers in eternity. But the Lord Jesus has never promised to answer all our questions. 'I am the way, the truth, and the life,' he says; 'no man cometh unto the Father but by me.' (St. John 14:6.) The great promise here is that if a man will come after Christ he will find a new life as he walks in Christ's way toward the truth which is God.

A research scientist starts out with a clue as his working hypothesis. If it is a sound clue, he receives one reassuring hint after another as his experiment proceeds. These hints come to him from the reality he is probing to let him know that he is moving on the right track. This is the normal pattern of scientific investigation. It is the constant pattern of the Christian investigation of God, which consists of taking Christ as one's clue to the meaning of existence and following it steadfastly, in face of all delays and frustrations and seeming contradictions. One of the most cogent vindications of the truth of Christianity is this very fact: that the further the Christian goes with his continuing act of faith in Christ as his clue, and the fiercer and more shattering grow the counter-attacks of the devil, the more assurance he is given that his clue is the right one—the only one that leads to the Father, to the ultimate truth at the heart of the universe and on its throne.

Chapter Nineteen

ENEMIES OF THE CROSS

III:17-19.

*Be imitators of me, brethren, and study those who live
in this way since you have us as an example. For, as I have told
you many times before and now with tears tell you again,
there are many who live as enemies of the cross of Christ. Their
end is destruction; their god is their belly; their glory is in*
their shame, and their minds are fixed on sordid matters.

Paul frankly recognizes that the Philippians are
still at a stage of spiritual development in which they must
rely upon imitating their betters, and there is danger that
they will take the wrong people as their pattern of Christian behavior. They are to imitate Paul rather than those
others, because he is a faithful, albeit imperfect, imitator of
Christ.

Our chief problem in this passage is the identity of
those *who live as enemies of the cross of Christ.* Whoever
they are, whatever their offense, they must be members of
the Christian Church. Paul would evince no such tearful
concern for Jews or pagans living as belly-worshipers. Nor
can they very well be the Judaizing Christians, who were
men of chaste life and genuine piety. Our inference is that

they are Christians who pervert Paul's doctrine of grace. They suppose that because God forgives the sinner and saves us by his grace rather than by our merits we can live as licentiously as we please, after the fashion of the cynical worldling who sins with an easy conscience, saying 'God will forgive me—that's his line.' They are antinomians, and probably of Gentile background, since Gentile Christians would be more inclined to this error than would Jewish Christians.

Are there such people actually within the Philippian congregation? It must be so; otherwise it is hard to see why Paul should mention them. But if we hold that this is an interpolated passage from an earlier letter it makes sense. The pride and joy in the Philippians which Paul expresses in the main body of the Letter is something that belongs to a time after such black spots have been blotted out. It is reasonable to surmise that there were many licentious antinomians in the Philippian church when this polemical passage was written, and that by the time Paul came to write the later epistle these people had either been cured of their error or had left the Church.

They are called *enemies of the cross of Christ* because there is nothing of the spirit of the cross in their living, the spirit of self-denying love for God and the brethren. Christ lived for God and others—and was crucified for it. These men live for the satisfaction of their own selves. *Their end is destruction* because their course of life leads in the opposite direction from eternal life. *Their god—*their *summum bonum,* the object of their supreme concern—*is their belly,* meaning their self-centered appetites as a whole. *Their glory is in their shame,* though it is not a shame of which they are ashamed. They glory in the very things that are destroying them. *Their minds are fixed on sordid matters.* Paul's phrase is 'earthly things' and we have paraphrased it at some risk of inaccuracy. The context seems to make clear that these 'earthly things' are sordid. His point is that a man becomes in his own being what he likes most and dwells upon. We become what our taste is; and he whose mind is full of sordid things becomes a sordid person. Paul cannot think of their fate without weeping.

⌐

We can only conjecture precisely whom Paul is talking about, as *enemies of the cross of Christ,* but we know what he is talking about. He is talking about sanctified indulgence, a religion of pleasing ourselves with the bland assumption that God is pleased to have it so. *Enemies of the cross of Christ* is a harsh epithet to apply to any who are Christians in any sense or degree. But the truth must be faced. The worst enemy of Christ is the Christian who professes the Lord Jesus with his lips, who gratefully claims that he is saved by the cross of Christ, and who lives without a cross of his own.

It is not necessary to assume that they whose *god is their belly,* whose *minds are fixed on sordid matters,* are gross sensualists, drunkards, gluttons, fornicators, open and obvious evil-livers. The 'belly' is the self; the 'sordid matters' are the concerns of self as opposed to the concerns of God. None the less, it is true that the man who does not live his life with the mind of Christ in him is a sensualist in the literal sense that he finds his treasure only in the things that can be grasped through the senses. This includes fine automobiles, a home with a 'good address,' financial security, costly collectors' items, no less than it includes gourmet's fare, a well-stocked private bar, and a mink-clothed mistress. Thoroughly respectable church members can be *enemies of the cross of Christ* without ever doing a thing that could be called immoral. The mystery of iniquity is at the core of every life of which Christ is not the center. And where this mystery abounds, human life is of the flesh and not of the spirit.

Paul says that the end of such people is destruction. His Greek word can be translated 'ruin.' This kind of materialism, which assumes that a man's true wealth is to be found in the things he possesses, is the ruination of the person because it prevents him from being what God designs and intends him to be: a Christ-like being. Christ does not despise material goods and pleasures; rather, he renounces them as the object of his desire and striving, and puts in their place the doing of the will of God. As he serves the Father's will, some material goods and pleasures come to him in the course of life, and he enjoys them. Jesus is not a pure ascetic, or indeed an ascetic at all in the accepted sense of the term. He enjoys eating, drinking, hospitality, social pleasures, all of the wholesome goods of human life as these come his way. Indeed, he enjoys them more keenly than does he who strives for them, because he accepts them and revels in them as gifts of the Father's love, whereas the worldly man grasps them anxiously as things which must be grabbed and gulped now before they pass—and worried about lest they escape. There is none of that fever of possession in Jesus, because the treasure of his heart is elsewhere.

The cross of Christ in Christian living is the renunciation of worldly goods as the primary object of desire and striving, with the joyful, loving acceptance of the Father's will as our primary object. It means the crucifixion of the old man, of our selfish nature with all its lusts and appetites. This inner death is no disaster, for it precedes and makes possible the birth of the new being in the radiant image of Christ. Man does not come into his true self until this death of the old and birth of the new have taken place. As I write these words, a large business building across the street is being demolished. This property was worth many millions of dollars, being located on Fifth Avenue in the heart of midtown Manhattan. Many months are required simply to tear it down. About two years are required for the building of the new thirty-eight-story office building which will replace it. The bystander's first thought is of the appalling waste of this vast operation. It is an excellent building they are tearing down. There can be no income from the property from the day when the old building becomes vacated until the day when the new one is put in use. The loss runs into many millions of dollars. But the men behind it all know what they are doing. They see this loss as the price they pay for the gain to come. It is not real loss at all, but the price of gain.

The cross of voluntary renunciation is the price to be paid for the glorious gain accruing to him who counts all things as loss in order to gain Christ and to share with him the true life which is life eternal: the life of perfect obedience to the Father's will. As for the material goods which are 'lost' in this exchange, it should be understood that this is the only way of 'gaining' even these.

It is instructive to recall Christ at the wedding feast in Cana (St. John 2:1-11). Here are the good things of this life in happy profusion: good food, good drink, good friends, and a good time. Christ enjoys this occasion as only he can—as only God can. Here the good things are, and God has provided them. Christ has not sought them or sweat for them; they come to him as an unsought gift, a pleasant surprise. It is when the good things of life come to us in this way, and we receive them in this way, that our joy in them is made full.

Chapter Twenty

COLONISTS OF HEAVEN

III:1, 20-21, IV:1.

Finally, my brothers, rejoice in the Lord... For our citizenship is established in heaven, whence we await a Saviour, the Lord Jesus Christ, who shall transform the body of our present low estate into conformity to the body of his glory by the working of his power, which is able to subdue all things to himself. So then, my brothers, whom I love and long for, my joy and crown, my dearly beloved, stand fast in the Lord in this way.

For reasons already given in Chapter Sixteen, we assume that verses 1b-19 are interpolated from an earlier letter, and that in the present letter the original sequence was from verse 1a to 20.

Rejoice in the Lord, because *our citizenship is established in heaven.* The metaphor is that used by Jesus in his words to the Seventy: 'Rejoice because your names are enrolled in heaven' (St. Luke 10:20). This means, as an older commentator puts it, that they are enrolled burgesses of the New Jerusalem. Paul is reminding the Philippians of why they cannot be perfectly conforming subjects of the Roman Empire, obeying any decree of Caesar regardless of what it demands of them. They have another and higher loyalty, obedience, and citizenship, in Christ's kingdom, not Caesar's.

The word we translate as 'citizenship' means 'state' or 'commonwealth.' Professor Moffatt's translation is superb: 'We are a colony of heaven.' Philippi was a colony of Rome; Christians anywhere are colonists of heaven. We find the same conception in Eph. 2:19 and Heb. 11:13ff. In the *Epistle to Diognetus* (second century) a Christian writer says of Christians that 'they pass their time upon earth, but they have their citizenship in heaven.'

In declaring that their citizenship *is established* in heaven Paul emphasizes the unshakable, eternal reality of their heavenly *patria*. This citizenship is not like Roman citizenship, merely temporal and transient, nor is it a pious 'daydream of the downtrodden,' to use Nietzsche's phrase. It is an exalted status which is theirs now and forever.

They possess it now, but the best is yet to be. *We await a Saviour, the Lord Jesus Christ.* The verb translated 'await' implies eager, intense expectation, with no hint of that patient passivity which our English word suggests. Jesus will come as *saviour* to his colonists on earth. Paul uses this term very rarely. He may be using it here as a claim for Christ against Caesar, for the Roman emperors were commonly called the saviours of their people. By acknowledging Christ as their king, the Christians put themselves outside the realm of the Roman saviour-emperor's protection. Paul reminds them that they have as their king the only invincible saviour, who comes not from Rome but from heaven—the realm of omnipotence.

He will come to save them—from what, and to what? Paul gives his answer in terms of the metamorphosis of our earthly body to the heavenly body that the Lord will give us at his coming. Paul's conception of the transmutation of the body in the resurrection is fully expounded in I Cor. 15:42-53. This will be accomplished *by the working of his power which is able to subdue all things to himself.*

Paul's idea of *the body of our present low estate* must not be taken as a disparagement of the natural body. The Authorized Version's reading, 'our vile body,' is incorrect and seriously misleading. Paul has in mind, not the viciousness of the body but its weakness. His point is that under the conditions of earthly life the Christian cannot serve God with perfect freedom, being subject as he is to all the ills that flesh is heir to: poverty, ignorance, pain, temptation, and death. From this bondage we shall be delivered by the divine Saviour, who at his coming will transform our body—our life as it is now lived—*into conformity to the body of his glory*, thus making us like himself not only in character but in power. Paul's vision is as one of the hymn-writers expresses it:

> *Oh, how glorious and resplendent,*
> *Fragile body, shalt thou be,*
> *When endowed with heavenly beauty,*
> *Full of health, and strong, and free,*

Full of vigor, full of pleasure
That shall last eternally. [1]

*So then, my brothers, whom I love and long for,
my joy and crown, my dearly beloved, stand fast in the
Lord in this way*—that is, buoyed up and sustained by this
hope and sure confidence of the coming salvation.

———

The resurrection of the body to the life everlasting
is a mystery of faith that cannot be subjected to strictly
rational analysis. The Christian believes in the resurrection
of the dead because he sees God in Christ, and God raising
Christ. He believes that God proposes to do with us what
he does with his Son crucified, dead, and buried. Hence the
resurrection event in Christ's life is decisive for the Christian's
conviction about his own destiny: because Christ
lives, he shall live also.

But the Christian has more than the original Easter
event to guarantee his own resurrection. After all, we could
believe that Christ rose from the dead without finding in
that any real assurance that we shall rise from our death.
There is another ground of our resurrection hope, something
that is very prominent in Paul's understanding of his
own experience in Christ: he sees his resurrection as already
begun, already in process. In such characteristic utterances

1. John Mason Neale's translation of a medieval Latin
hymn.

as 'Christ liveth in me' (Gal. 2:20) he expresses his awareness that God has begun in him that transposition from
temporal to eternal life which will be completed beyond
death.

In the claim that *our citizenship is established in
heaven* Paul is not talking about glorious things to come
but about glorious things present. Already the Christian
enjoys this supernal citizenship in his heavenly patria. The
Roman citizen living in one of the colonies may be far from
the imperial city, but where he is Rome is. This seems to
be something for the non-Roman to envy, but what a poor
beggarly thing it is—says Paul—compared to what *we* have!
And we know that we have it, because do we not feel the
power of our King whenever we call upon him? Christ is
with us, at all times, in all places. He lives in us, and we in
him; and our resurrection has begun, the great change that
will make us ready for the glories which eye cannot now
see nor ear hear nor tongue speak.

But all we know now is the beginning. A day will
come when the initiation will be ended and the full life will
begin. It matters little what Paul and his Christian con-
temporaries had in mind as they contemplated that day. As
the primitive Christian eschatology faded, Christians came
to think of the day of the Lord as the day in each person's
life when he dies to this present world. Thus we normally
think of it today, while we retain the substance of the
Lord's own teaching in our creedal assertion that he shall
come again with glory to judge the quick and the dead.

We need to be saved from two present afflictions: sin and death. Throughout his writings Paul links these twin enemies very closely together. His primary concern in the present passage is with death, our condition of mortality. Our sorrow is not simply that we die, but that in this mortal state we are so powerless to do the things God moves us to do. Our sin is not our only handicap as servants of God. Our poverty, our ignorance, our ineptitude, our bodily frailties, our involvement in a sinful human society, our shortness of time, our growing old and the progressive loss of such powers as we have: these are among the burdens of *the body of our present low estate*. They are humiliating and frustrating. From them we long to be delivered. And from them, in the Lord's good time, we shall be delivered *by the working of his power which is able to subdue all things unto himself.*

We turn to Paul's great fifteenth chapter of First Corinthians for a fuller presentation of his concept. This *body of our present low estate* 'is sown in corruption; it is raised in incorruption: it is sown in dishonor; it is raised in glory: it is sown in weakness; it is raised in power: it is sown a natural body; it is raised a spiritual body' (I Cor. 15:42-44). It would be easy and natural, but wrong, to consider all this as referring to the death of the body. Paul has in mind rather the birth in us of the new man in Christ. The new man is 'sown'—born—'in corruption,' the corruption of our tainted human nature; born in the dishonor and the weakness of human life. But the new man is destined to a mighty conquest and transcendence of all its present limitations. He is already on his way toward that victory. The death of his natural body—his death to what we call nature —will be his birth into eternity and his entrance upon a mode of being in which his body will be like Christ's eternal body in glory, in power, and in capacity to serve God's purposes without any let or hindrance from the frailties of mortal flesh.

The Revised Standard Version well translates I Cor. 15:48: 'As was the man of dust, so are those who are of the dust; and as is the man of heaven [meaning Christ], so are those who are of heaven.'[2] We are 'of heaven' if we are in Christ. Whatever pains we must now bear are the growth pains of a life that is endless and destined to glory inconceivable.

Such is Paul's fundamental faith in man under God and in Christ. This present life is no blind alley or dead-end street. Death is an episode in the unfolding of life. When the darkness of earth's fleeting day closes in from behind us, the light of dawning eternity breaks in front of us, and we lie down, not to pleasant dreams, but to passage from weakness to strength, from faith to sight, from struggle to fulfillment. Death is not banished; it is swallowed up in victory.

2. From the *Revised Standard Version of the Bible*, copyrighted 1946 and 1952 by the Division of Christian Education, National Council of Churches. Used by permission.

Chapter Twenty-one

WHEN SAINTS CAN'T CLICK

IV:2-3.

I entreat Euodia and Syntyche, both, to be of one mind in the Lord. Yea, I beg you, true yoke-fellow, to help those women who have labored at my side in the work of the Gospel, along with Clement and my other fellow workers whose names are in the Book of Life.

There have been some ingenious guesses as to the identity of Euodia and Syntyche. One theory holds that they are not persons but parties. The Authorized Version regards the former as a man, rendering the name as Euodias. Theodore of Mopsuestia (fourth century) made the latter a man, with the masculine name Syntyches. Tyndale and Cranmer held this view, and Grotius thought that both were men. The text as we have it indicates clearly that both were women.

The reasonable assumption is that they were two excellent Christian ladies who had trouble clicking with one another. Paul entreats them *to be of one mind in the Lord*. If they cannot be of one opinion on the point at issue between them, they can be of one mind and work together amicably if they submerge their differences in a common devotion to Christ.

He begs an unnamed friend, his *true yokefellow*, to use his good influence with these women to reconcile them. Here is another mystery man. Clement of Alexandria supposed that it was Paul's wife, and Renan added the romantic detail that Paul's wife was Lydia! Other guesses have suggested Barnabas, Luke, Silas, Timothy and Epaphroditus. Moffatt maintains the more plausible theory that the Greek word *synzyge*, 'yoke-fellow,' is really a proper name: Synzygos. This could be a name that some Christian took at baptism.

Whoever he is, Paul asks him to help these women to compose their difference. They are well worth the effort, since they *have labored at my side in the work of the Gospel*.

The mention of *Clement and my other fellow workers* evidently alludes to some experience well known to Paul and 'Synzygos.'

The reference to *the Book of Life* in which these workers' names are written is the only instance of it in the New Testament outside of the Apocalypse. It means that God keeps an imperishable record of his faithful servants, and none can be forgotten.

The old doggerel verse is only too true:

To live with the saints in heaven
Is bliss and glory.
To live with the saints on earth
Is often another story.

Euodia and Syntyche are authentic saints, not grand dames or dilettantes who take a little religion for the sake of appearances or to make them feel good. They have worked, fought, sacrificed, and suffered alongside of Paul in the work of the Gospel. They have counted not their lives dear unto themselves. But their personal feud is bitter enough to call for Paul's special attention from far away and for the *true yoke-fellow's* reconciling help.

We cannot 'stack our personalities at the door of the church' when we come in. We must carry everything that is in us into our worship of God and our service of Christ, and that includes those things in us that are not too loving and not too lovable. Our Lord must use us whether we are agreeable, co-operative, easy to get along with or not. The problem of Euodia and Syntyche is found wherever two or three are gathered together in Christ's name, and the world is not always forced to say: 'Behold, how these Christians love one another.' Sometimes we give it too good cause to say, 'Behold, how these Christians wrangle and bicker.'

But perhaps it is better so. Christ wants us to bring our whole selves, the best and the worst in us, into his community of love and labor—so that our whole selves can be transformed into his likeness. We should note well that he does not command us to be of one opinion about anything, or of one taste; his command it that we be, in Paul's phrase, *of one mind* in him—the mind of love. This is what Euodia and Syntyche need to be brought to, as do all Christians. It may be that their very zeal for the Gospel has exacerbated the difference between them. This can easily happen. Christians who care little for the Lord's cause find it easy to get along with one another. Much that passes for noble tolerance is only bland indifference. It is when people care intensely for something bigger than themselves that they are tempted to be annoyed intensely by others who share their devotion.

There is only one antidote to this mutual animosity engendered by a common concern for a common cause. It is to care more, not less, for the Lord himself—*to be of one mind in the Lord*. It always works when it is applied. We appreciate one another as we see how our Lord appreciates the other. We care for one another as we see how the Lord cares for the other. We are all brethren: but it is only as we have in us the mind of Christ toward each other that we can live that truth.

Chapter Twenty-two

THE PROTECTING PEACE

IV:4-8.

Rejoice in the Lord at all times. I say it again, rejoice!
Let your gentleness be apparent to all men. The Lord is at
hand. Worry about nothing, but in every prayer and supplica-
tion make your needs known to God thankfully; and the peace
of God, which is beyond all human conception, shall protect
your hearts and thoughts in Christ Jesus.

*R**ejoice in the Lord at all times.* Paul's empha-
sis is upon the unbroken constancy of the Christian's joy in
the Lord—at all times, in all situations. There can never be
a moment even in this troubled life when the Christian
cannot rejoice. *In the Lord:* Christ risen and reigning is the
Christian's constant atmosphere.

Let your gentleness be apparent to all men. The
key word here is of elusive meaning. The Authorized
Version uses 'forbearance,' in line with Aristotle's use of
the word in his *Nichomachean Ethics*, where he uses it to
designate the temper of the man who never demands more
than his just due and will take even less for the sake of peace
and order. 'Moderation' would be the best English expression of this sense of the word. Paul may have in mind the
Christian's forbearance under persecution. On the evidence,

136

'gentleness' seems to be the best English rendition. They are to let this spirit in them *be apparent to all men*, both their pagan neighbors and their active persecutors. It is to be their way of manifesting the power of Christ in them.

The Lord is at hand. There are two alternative ways of taking this statement, but they do not conflict. It can mean (a) 'The Lord is near you at all times to bless and strengthen you,' or (b) 'The Lord is coming soon.' This can be a deliberate *double entendre*, with the meaning: 'You can be patient and forbearing under persecution, because you have the Lord with you to uphold you by his grace; and the time is not long until he comes to terminate the evil and diadem the right.'

Worry about nothing, but in every prayer and supplication make your needs known to God thankfully. Even in our direst need, when our prayers are most supplicatory, we are to pray *thankfully*—mindful not only of our need but of God's past and present bountiful supplying of all our needs. The recollection of God's goodness and loving-kindness to us throughout our days is the sure solvent of all anxiety.

And the peace of God, which is beyond all human conception, shall protect your hearts and thoughts in Christ Jesus. Nobody can begin to understand the peace of God. Its paradoxical quality we have considered in an earlier chapter (page 24f.). Paul is now suggesting that we shall receive this mysterious and glorious peace, not by trying to master its mystery by intellectual comprehension or by striving for it as an end in itself, but by the life of faith, obedience, and unceasing thankful prayer. When you have given your lives over to God in Christ, the peace of God *shall protect your hearts and thoughts in Christ Jesus.* Paul's verb is a word normally used when speaking of an armed garrison protecting a city. The peace of God is the divine garrison of the faithful soul amidst all the hostile powers which sorely beset it. *Hearts and thoughts* are the affections and the intelligence of man. The Christian is 'safe' from the world so long as his love and his thinking are centered upon his Lord. The Peace of God is the mighty fortress of the Christ-centered life.

I cannot find anywhere in the Bible or in all literature a more majestically peaceful figure than that of Christ before Pilate, as the fourth Gospel records the scene (St. John 19:5-14). Pilate, by contrast, is a very troubled soul. One wonders why. He is not the defendant but the judge. He is on the judge's seat, not in chains on the pavement. He will go home that night to a good dinner and a good sleep (or will he?). Why shouldn't he be peaceful? But he isn't. The man before him is bloody from the beating the soldiers have given him. An ugly crown of thorns has been pressed into his flesh. He has not a friend in sight; the God he trusted in has apparently forsaken him; and very shortly he will be nailed to a cross. Why should he be peaceful? But he is.

Pilate is perplexed by this curious situation, and acutely aware of it. He wonders if the prisoner is fully sane. Does he realize the real state of affairs—that Pilate has the power to order him killed or released, and that he himself has no power but to accept the verdict? Christ's answer illuminates the whole mystery: 'You could have no power against me, unless it were given to you from above.' The power to crucify him comes from God; but he knows God!

It is a most important truth about the passion of Christ. The power that crucifies Christ comes from God the Father, not from the devil. And as Christ faces the cross he recalls this and the peace of God holds him in its mighty embrace. The power of God, misused by men, will crucify him; but the love of God will have the last word, and it has power to turn the worst that men can do into victory over death and hell. Christ's mind is kept in perfect peace because he knows God.

He gives this invincible peace to his followers, by giving them the true knowledge of the true God. All power comes from God, even the power that is used to our hurt by man or the devil. We must understand, first and always, that power never has its origin in any evil source. Cancer, poverty, ignorance, war, sin, disease, the world's failure to understand us, our own failures, all such evils can trouble us; but they cannot conquer us, they cannot destroy our peace, so long as we fully realize that their power to hurt us belongs to the God who has all power—including the power to save us.

139

The peace of God is peace *with* God, the loving knowledge of him and harmony with him that enables us to put our whole being in his hands, knowing that no cross we suffer is final.

One of the noblest paeans to the peace of God is Henry Vaughan's exquisite poem *Peace*:

> *My Soul, there is a country*
> *Far beyond the stars,*
> *Where stands a wingèd sentry*
> *All skillful in the wars:*
> *There above noise, and danger,*
> *Sweet Peace sits crowned with smiles,*
> *And One born in a manger*
> *Commands the beauteous files.*
> *He is thy gracious Friend,*
> *And—O my Soul, awake!—*
> *Did in pure love descend*
> *To die here for thy sake.*
> *If thou canst get but thither,*
> *There grows the flower of Peace,*
> *The Rose that cannot wither,*
> *Thy fortress, and thy ease.*
> *Leave then thy foolish ranges,*
> *For none can thee secure*
> *But One, Who never changes,*
> *Thy God, thy life, thy cure.*

Anybody who would criticize this must do so on bended knee. But in one respect it does not do full justice to the peace of God which passes all human conception. 'If thou canst get but thither' suggests that we must climb from earth to heaven to reach the Peace. As for comparing it to a rose, a rose is as delicate and fragile as it is beautiful. 'There above noise, and danger, Sweet Peace sits crowned with smiles.' But the peace of God possesses the embattled soldier of Christ in the very thick of noise and danger. Vaughan rightly sees it as a heavenly treasure, but he fails to see, or at least to say, that the peace of God goes with the trusting child of God even as he descends into hell.

There is no peace to him who is at war with God. To him who is at peace with God there is nothing except peace.

Chapter Twenty-three

THE LIFE YOU LIVE IN YOUR MIND

IV:8-9.

As for the rest, brethren: whatever things are true, and worthy of reverence, and just, and pure, and lovely, and well spoken of, if there is any virtue and any praiseworthiness in these things fix your minds upon them. The things you have learned and received, and heard and seen, in me, do; and the God of peace shall be with you.

P aul here follows the literary device of the pagan moralists in drawing up a catalogue of virtues. Some of the virtues he names are identical with those praised by high-minded pagans. The Christian's goodness of character is not totally unlike that of any other man.

Whatever things are true. Things that may be appealing, or comforting, or charming, but which cannot meet the test of simple truth, are to be shunned. Our only friend is truth.

Whatever things are worthy of reverence: eloquent of the God who gives them. Most of the sacred things we experience are in the personal realm and shine forth from holy lives. But a sunset, or hymn, or a beautiful sanctuary, or anything that conveys to us the loving holiness of God, is worthy of reverence. God alone is to be worshiped; but anything that reveals him to us is sacred as a means and instrument by which he shows his glory to us.

Whatever things are pure. Purity, in the New Testament, is not exclusively identifiable with sexual chastity. That is pure which is not mixed or adulterated with elements which can debase the soul by drawing us away from God. If in Christian thought and speech 'impurity' has come to be peculiarly associated with sexual sin, it is for the very solid reason that sex so easily becomes the kind of obsession which excludes God and the things of God from the life that is given over to it.

Whatever things are just. Christian and pagan at their best share the sense of justice. Let no Christian come behind the noblest pagan in his passion for justice and righteousness.

Whatever things are lovely—that is, attractive. Paul's word means that which inspires love. The lovely thing is that which is worthy to be loved. A beautiful but evil thing cannot be lovely in this sense.

Whatever things are well spoken of, by people whose opinion is worth considering. This is not an undiscriminating endorsement of anything and everything that happens to be popular.

If there is any virtue and any praise-worthiness in these things fix your mind upon them. This is the only place where Paul speaks of *virtue,* the subject which was the chief preoccupation of the pagan moralist. He wants to lay it upon their minds that to be a Christian does not relieve one of the necessity of being a good person in the sense understood by all good and noble minds.

The things you have learned and received, and heard and seen, in me, do. A repetition of his frequent admonition to imitate him. *And the God of peace shall be with you,* as surely as God has been with him. This is a return to the great promise of the peace of God spoken in verse 7.

We think nowadays of psychology as a modern science. It is nothing of the kind. It is neither a science, in the precise sense of that term, nor modern. Sound psychology is the knowledge of what works for the health of man in his inner being; and such knowledge as we have of this tremendously important matter was ancient when Paul wrote this paragraph on mental health.

The working principle of all sound psychotherapy is as Paul enunciates it: *think on these things* that are good for us. Dwell upon them lovingly, imaginatively, gratefully, and the virtue that is in them penetrates your being and becomes part of yourself. The soul is dyed in the color of that which it habitually contemplates. As a man thinketh in his heart, so is he.

When a person is sick in mind and spirit, hence in his central self, his vital interest, attention, and desire must be redirected from the wrong objects to the right ones. We can perfect new techniques of helping people to do this, though we should note well that no psychotherapist using any technique can help anybody except as the patient wants to be helped. This *wanting* to be healed and changed is the first requisite. If any good is to be done, this desire must be present in force.

Christianity provides this necessary longing and desire to be changed. To be a Christian in the depth of one's being is to want to be like Jesus Christ, to hunger and thirst for the perfect righteousness—rightness of being—which is in him. Paul the convert is writing to fellow converts at Philippi. These people have given up all for the sake of being Christians. Their supreme desire in life is to be conformed to Christ in their own being. So the intense desire to be changed is powerfully operative in them, and all that their teacher has to do is to remind them of how this is to be done: by fixing and keeping their minds on the things good, true, and lovely, whose qualities they want to make part of themselves.

It is well recognized in our day that a strong Christian faith and devotion can provide this sufficient desire for change which one must have, but the general recognition of this has led many people into a serious error. The error lies in supposing that we can use Christianity as prescriptive medicine for what ails people. It says such things as this: 'If you will take up Christianity you will find it immensely helpful toward achieving peace of mind, a positive approach to life, a healthy personality.' 'If the nations of the world would only become Christian and make the Sermon on the Mount the constitution of the new world, we could scrap our armies and navies and become a happy world family.' Such assertions are usually true, as assertions; but they badly confuse the issue. We cannot become Christians in order to become better people. We can only, as Christians, strive to become better people so that we can be better Christians. Surely this is no quibble. Nobody can become a Christian as a means to some other end. We can be Christians only if we have answered the call of God to give up all for the sake of Jesus Christ *regardless of what it might do to us.* The aspiring Christian who, with God's help, is striving to become Christ-like is a very healthy and happy person indeed compared to other men. But his psychic health is the by-product of his passionate striving for Christ-likeness.

The Christian has his own 'inscape'—to use a word of Christopher Morley's. Your landscape is what you see outside yourself, your external world. Your inscape is what you see with 'that inward eye which is the bliss of solitude.' When Hanns Lilje, the courageous German Evangelical pastor, was imprisoned by the Nazis, he kept not only his faith but his sanity alive by the use of his inscape. In his book of witness, *The Valley of the Shadow,* he relates:

'I made a strictly ordered rule-of-life for each day, which included regular meditation and prolonged periods of prayer, followed by periods of thought on theological and ecclesiastical questions. The result of these reflections

146

helps me in my work today. Since I had no paper to write down the result of my thinking I not only repeated it over and over again, in order to impress it upon my memory, but I also frequently translated my thoughts into English, or French, or even into Latin, and this, in itself, did my memory a great deal of good. Under these circumstances, I could only repeat passages from the Bible, and verses from the hymn-book, which I had retained in my memory. How grateful I am to all my teachers who had made me learn by heart hymns and poems, Greek lyrics, Latin odes, or Hebrew psalms! They provided me with a treasure which in those hard days was literally priceless.'([1])

This man had the advantage of an unusually well-stocked mind, providing a rich intellectual inscape. Most of us lack his equipment in that respect. But we all have some supply of such goods in our memories, and we can all be building up our supply and using it daily.

But the focus and center of our inscape should be Christ himself, so that at all times and in all places we can feed on him in our hearts, by faith, with thanksgiving. *Whatever things are true, worthy of reverence, just, pure, lovely,* and *well spoken of* all shine with their brightest luster in him. To carry him in our minds and to fix our minds and affections upon him is to become as he is. When this is the life we live in our minds, we are given to know that it is the life eternal.

1. Lilje, Hanns, *The Valley of the Shadow*, Philadelphia, 1950, p. 55. By permission of The Muhlenberg Press, publishers.

Chapter Twenty-four

TAKING ALL THINGS IN STRIDE

IV:10-20

I rejoice heartily in the Lord that now you have revived your concern for me, which undoubtedly you felt before but you lacked opportunity to act upon it. Not that I complain about being in want, for I have learned to be content in any circumstances whatever. I know how to be in need and I know how to be in plenty. In everything and in all things I have learned how to eat and how to go hungry, how to have plenty and how to have little. In him who strengthens me I can meet anything. None the less, you did well to share my affliction with me. You know that you Philippians, in the early days of the Gospel when I left Macedonia, were the only church that shared with me in giving and receiving, for even when I was in Thessalonika both once and twice you sent what I needed. I do not seek the gift, but I seek the fruit which abounds to your credit. I have all I need, and more; I am full of the good things I have received from you by the hand of Epaphroditus, 'an odor of fragrance,' a sacrifice acceptable and pleasing to God. My God will meet all your need, according to his wealth in glory, in Christ Jesus. Unto God and our Father be glory forever and ever. Amen.

Now, before bringing his letter to a close, Paul chooses to return to the subject of their past kindness and concern for him. Although he has mentioned it in 1:5, here for the first time he expresses his thanks formally and fully. Some commentators sense a self-defensive note in this passage: Paul is asserting his independence of all human support in reply to some who have charged that he lives on the charity of the Church. It may be so, but it is not a necessary assumption. The surface meaning of his words is simply that he is happy to have received their gift, not so much for his own sake as for theirs, because *I seek the fruit which abounds to your credit.* In ministering to him they minister to Christ and they show their true citizenship of God's kingdom.

The fact that he expresses his thanks to them at the close of the Letter rather than at the beginning may mean that he had earlier written a note of thanksgiving.

I rejoice heartily in the Lord that now you have revived your concern for me, which undoubtedly you felt before but you lacked opportunity to act upon it. Circumstances, or sheer poverty on their part, had prevented it. This is a puzzling statement. If their concern for him has been felt all along, it is strange that he should speak of its being *revived* at this time. He means, apparently, that now their concern is able to act, as it could not before. This is its revival. Perhaps they now had money previously lacking; perhaps there was somebody now who could bring their contribution to him.

Lest anybody suppose that he cannot get along without the material aid of his brethren, he goes on to assert: *Not that I complain about being in want, for I have learned now to be content in any circumstances whatever. I know how to be in need and I know how to be in plenty. In everything and in all things I have learned how to eat and how to go hungry, how to have plenty and how to have little.* There is unmistakable vehemence in this protestation, as though he wants to make sure that the most sceptical will understand. He is not dependent upon handouts from anybody; he is dependent only upon the Lord. His word that we translate 'content' is a word commonly used by Stoic philosophers to mean 'independent,' 'self-sufficing.' It was a cardinal tenet of Stoicism that a man's only true resources were within himself, never in external things and circumstances. Paul would agree with the Stoic about the external things and circumstances, but he has a totally different idea of the source of a man's sufficiency. The Stoic says, 'I can meet anything in the courage and rectitude of my own soul.' Paul says *In him who strengthens me I can meet anything.* His sufficiency is of God.

Once again Paul uses the language of the Mysteries. *In everything and in all things I have learned*—his Greek word means 'initiated into the secret of'—*how to eat and how to go hungry* ... He who has mastered this secret belongs to the fully initiated in the Mystery of Christ.

In him who strengthens me I can meet anything. Oliver Cromwell said that this verse once saved his life. When his eldest son died, he was nearly crushed by despair. Then he discovered this verse and exclaimed 'He that was Paul's Christ is my Christ too!' It put him on his feet again.

It is here that Paul differs *toto caelo* from the Stoics. He finds his strength not in himself but in his vital union with Christ.

None the less, you did well to share my affliction with me. However independent of man's help Paul may be, by virtue of his being in Christ, the fact that they helped him and shared his trouble with him is cause for rejoicing because it is proof that they too are in Christ. The mark and sign of the man in Christ is his bearing the burdens of others.

You know that you Philippians, in the early days of the Gospel when I left Macedonia, were the only church that shared with me in giving and receiving, for even when I was in Thessalonika both once and twice you sent what I needed. Our translation is quite free, to bring out the meaning. Paul says literally, 'And you know, Philippians, that in the beginning of the Gospel, when I left Macedonia, no other church shared with me in giving and receiving except you alone . . .' *In the early days of the Gospel* refers to the first time of his association with them, not to the beginning of his ministry, which was many years before that. *You . . . were the only church that shared with me in giving and receiving.* The language is financial, meaning: 'You were the only church that did business with me.' They gave him material help, he gave them spiritual gifts; hence his relationship to them was one of giving and receiving on both sides. *Even when I was in Thessalonika both once and twice you sent what I needed.* After his first visit to Philippi, Paul had gone directly to the seaport of Thessalonika. He is saying here that he was hardly out of their sight before receiving several gifts from them.

I do not seek the gift, but I seek the fruit which abounds to your credit. Financial language again. The 'fruit' of an investment is its interest and dividends. The Philippians have 'invested' in Paul, and the dividends are heavenly and eternal. He rejoices for their sake that they have done so.

I have all I need, and more! I am full of the good things I have received from you by the hand of Epaphroditus, 'an odor of fragance,' a sacrifice acceptable and pleasing to God. They have given him joy by showing him that they have mastered the great secret of the life in Christ that it is more blessed to give than to receive. In calling their offering *'an odor of fragrance,' a sacrifice acceptable and pleasing to God* Paul uses liturgical language that would make sense to Christians with either a Jewish or a Gentile background. *'An odor of fragrance'* is a phrase used a number of times in the Old Testament. Though their offering is a gift to him, it is still more a gift to God, hence a sacrifice.

My God will meet all your need, according to his wealth in glory, in Christ Jesus. Unto God and our Father be glory forever and ever. Amen. When we care for others, we discover as we never could otherwise God's care for us, his supplying all our material and spiritual

152

needs *according to his wealth in glory, in Christ Jesus*. This clause is not easy to interpret. God's *wealth* is clear enough; but what shall we make of *in glory, in Christ Jesus?* We can best explain *in Christ Jesus* by linking it with God's meeting of our need: he meets our need through Christ, the mediator of God's goodness to man. The word *glory* may have been inserted wrongly by a copyist who saw it in the following verse. *In glory* can be an adverbial phrase meaning 'gloriously'; or it may be eschatological, referring to the glorious consummation of the coming age. The approximate sense is, 'My God in his wealth will gloriously meet all your need through Jesus Christ.'

Unto God and our Father be glory forever and ever. Amen. This doxology brings the Letter to a formal close, but a few words of personal greeting will be added.

↤

One who has read Mackinlay Kantor's *Andersonville*, that grim study of an inglorious phase of the American civil war, will not soon forget how the author portrays the horrible shrinking and dehumanization of souls suffering in the prison camp. The process is traced in one life after another. One may want to take issue with Mr. Kantor's underlying thesis, that most people go to pieces as people and sink into bestiality when they are treated as beasts. But his novel, even though it is fiction, is abundantly documented. It is substantially true, and its truth, unfortunately, is not restricted to one time, place, and human cast in the drama of history. Most people of anytime and anywhere can be decent only when their circumstances favor their decency.

I have learned how to be content in any circumstances whatever, says Paul; *I know how to be in need and I know how to be in plenty* . . . And then his reason: *In him who strengthens me I can meet anything.*

In earlier chapters we have explored Paul's faith under fire and we have seen how he welcomed adversity as a God-sent opportunity to serve his Lord in some way that would not otherwise be possible. There is no need to review that testimony here. It may be useful simply to observe how Paul's faith enables him to take all things in stride as they come to him. When he is free, he can visit Philippi and Thessalonika and every place where he is needed. But imprisonment does not throw him off stride. It enables him to do something else: to preach his Gospel to the soldiery. Every new thing as it comes to him discloses a new directive of the Lord: 'You have been doing thus-and-so; now I want you to turn to something else.' It will go on this way to the end. When the end comes, he will hear the Lord say: 'I have asked you to live for me. Now I ask you to die for me.' This, too, he will do in stride.

In a famous Christian epigram Lord Bacon notes that 'prosperity is the blessing of the Old Testament; adversity is the blessing of the New; which carrieth the greater benediction, and the clearer revelation of God's favour.' In Chapter six we examined the distinctly Christian reasoning about adversity as the greater benediction. Genuine faith and devotion alone can make this reasoning reasonable.

Faith has many facets, and many vital implications. We should note one in particular, as we contemplate Paul's marvelous ability to take all things in stride. This is faith's proposition that our experience at any given moment is only an episode in the whole story of our eternal career under God. The present tribulation is never the end. Nothing is ever the end. There is always more to come, and how we handle the present crisis will have a permanent, even an eternal, effect upon our future. Paul hungering or cast out or in prison knows that he will not hunger or suffer forever, but while he is in this present moment he must let the Lord make the maximum use of him. One much closer to us in time, Sir Wilfred Grenfell, demonstrated as robust a faith as any saint, throughout his long career as a medical missionary in Labrador. One experience seemed to be the end of him, but he lived to tell about it. He had set out with his dog team on a sick call which took him over the frozen water of an ocean bay. While he was on his way the ice broke up, and he found himself with his team and sled on a floating island of ice drifting out to sea. He mercifully put his huskies to death, fashioned a coat for himself from their hides, contrived a distress flag, and then lay down and slept. The improbable happened and he was rescued. Some one asked him later how, under these frightening conditions, he could so calmly go to sleep. He answered, 'There was nothing to fear. I had done all I could. Certainly I had done all that was *humanly* possible. The rest lay in God's hands. What, then, was there to be afraid of?'

The person who can take such a crisis in stride is not necessarily a natural hero. All that is required of him, but this is absolutely required, is that he know, with all his heart and soul and mind and strength, that he is now and forever in God's hands; that God has a special work for him in every new situation; and that this is not the end, but a link in the chain of his eternal destiny.

Chapter Twenty-five

SAINTS OF CAESAR'S HOUSEHOLD

IV:21-23.

Greet every saint in Christ Jesus. The brethren who are with me greet you. All the saints greet you, especially they who are of Caesar's household. The grace of the Lord Jesus Christ be with your spirit.

It is surprising and disappointing that Paul's personal greetings at the end of this letter to his favorite church are not more specific. Why he does not mention some of them by name, as at the close of *Romans* and other letters, we cannot tell.

The brethren who are with me want to be remembered to the Philippians. It need not be assumed that they knew personally the Christians at Philippi. They who are in Christ can greet their brethren affectionately without knowing them personally, because in Christ all are brethren.

They who are of Caesar's household are not necessarily members of the Imperial family, and most probably are not. The term 'Caesar's household' was used very broadly to include all who were in the Emperor's service, either as slaves or as civil servants.

The closing benediction, *the grace of the Lord*

Jesus Christ be with your spirit, seems at a glance to be simply a conventional blessing, but one detail calls for special notice: the blessing is invoked upon their collective *spirit* rather than upon their individual spirits. The Christian *esprit de corps* is a corporate reality, making all members one in God and with each other.

⌁

The allusion to the Christians *of Caesar's household* opens to our view an impressive and dramatic human situation. Here are slaves and employees of the Emperor, bound by their position to be against anything that Caesar was against. Here is Paul, the notorious leader of the subversive Christian movement, which was considered a deadly menace to the Roman order. And here are these members of the Imperial staff secretly stealing away in their spare moments to the dungeon where their beloved Paul awaits trial for sedition.

We are not to suppose that among them are sons and daughters of Nero, or senators, or society matrons, although this is by no means impossible. The fact is impressive enough without that. These people have everything to gain by being 100 per cent-Romans and Caesarites, everything to lose by being Christians. Yet Christians they are. They put principle above policy, love above life, Christ above Caesar.

As we reflect critically upon the behavior of such

early Christians we are bound to ask if their secrecy was honorable. The truth is that they were living a double life, they were practicing concealment. Would it not have been more consistent with their heavenly calling to have come right out with an open profession of their allegiance to the outlawed Christ? It is a fair question, but in answering it we must be fair to them. Christ himself practiced secrecy, and enjoined it upon others, until the time came when open and public self-declaration was in order. The early Christian code required that a Christian must tell the whole truth when the question was put to him: 'Are you a Christian?' None of those saints of Caesar's household would have specifically denied his Christian allegiance, if he was loyal to the code. But the time was not ripe for an open profession of Christianity, except under questioning. The Holy Spirit was their guide and counselor in this matter. This was a time for being wise as serpents; for Christianity was a revolutionary movement in that situation, as it is in any situation, and at the time of Paul's imprisonment the movement was only beginning.

Prudent they were, but not cowardly prudent. They were risking all for Christ's sake, and what could they expect to get in return? The Lord's promise to such is plain: 'Houses, and brethren, and sisters, and mothers, and children, and lands'—all these they shall have here and now—'with persecutions; and in the world to come eternal life.' (St. Mark 10: 30.) Jesus promises his sworn followers that they will 'have'—spiritually possess and enjoy—all the good things of this world, 'with persecutions,' and in the world to come eternal life.

The Christian principle is that we never truly possess a thing until we renounce it. He who gives up the world for Christ's sake receives it back from God's hands in such a way that he now has the freedom to enjoy it, without being burdened any longer by the anxiety of claiming and owning it. When the Christians gather in Paul's cell to pray, sing, and eat together, they enjoy what they have as Nero in his palace can enjoy nothing. They have 'brothers, and sisters, and mothers, and children, and lands' in their household of faith and family of love.

The Christians in Rome send their affectionate greetings to the Christians in Philippi whom they do not know. But they do know them, and love them, and belong to them, because they all belong to the Christ who is their common love and common life.

All these good things they have 'with persecutions.' Christ bids us rejoice when we are persecuted for his sake, but he does not say that such persecution is in itself a good thing. Let there be no pretense about this. Christians are persecuted because the world hates Christ; and it hurts to be persecuted. Christ recognizes that 'the world to come' has not yet come, and until it comes his faithful ones must suffer with him. Our rejoicing under persecution is to be for the proof this persecution gives that we are really standing for Christ, and strongly enough to deserve being persecuted.

'And in the world to come eternal life.' The Johannine tradition in the New Testament makes much of the fact that eternal life begins here and now, rather than putting it wholly into the eternal future. There is no real contradiction between St. John and the synoptic Gospels on this point. The Christ of St. Mark is saying that in the world to come our eternal life will be freed from all pain of persecution and from all fetters of earthly circumstance.

So, for Paul and the saints of Caesar's household, for Timothy and the Philippians and all of Christ's people of any time and place, true life begins when all life is surrendered and given over to God in Christ.

> *Let goods and kindred go,*
> *This mortal life also.*
> *The body they may kill;*
> *God's truth abideth still:*
>   *His kingdom is forever.*

Somehow, Luther's stirring words leave one great word unspoken. It is not only God's truth which abideth still, when we live and die in its service. We ourselves abide still. 'The world passeth away, and the lust thereof: but *he that doeth the will of God abideth forever.*' (1 St. John 2:17.) The words are St. John's, but the faith is St. Paul's, and every Christian's who believes in the Lord in truth and has given up all to follow him.

AUTHOR'S TRANSLATION OF THE LETTER

THE LETTER OF PAUL THE APOSTLE
TO THE PHILIPPIANS

CHAPTER I

(1) Paul and Timothy, slaves of Jesus Christ, to all the faithful in Christ Jesus who are at Philippi, with the bishops and deacons: (2) grace and peace to you from God our Father and from the Lord Jesus Christ.

(3) I thank my God whenever I remember you, (4) and constantly in all my prayers I intercede for you all with joy (5) because of your fellowship with me in the Gospel from the first day to the present. (6) As I do this I am confident of one thing: that he who has begun a good work in you will follow through with it until the day of Jesus Christ.

(7) It is right that I should think this about you all, since I have you all in my heart as sharers of grace with me, both in my chains and in my defense and strengthening of the Gospel. (8) God is my witness that I long for you all in the very heart of Christ Jesus. (9) I pray above all that your

love may increase more and more, in accurate knowledge and all true discernment, (10) so that you will approve all things that matter most and you will be sincere and blameless to the very day of Jesus Christ, (11) filled with the fruit of that righteousness which comes from Jesus Christ and is to the glory and praise of God.

(12) I want you to know, brethren, that these things that have happened to me serve for the advancement of the Gospel, (13) since my imprisonment as a Christian is a fact known throughout the whole palace guard and by everybody else; (14) and most of our brethren have been made bolder by it, so that they dare to proclaim the word of God more courageously.

(15) Some indeed preach Christ out of envy and rivalry, and others out of genuine good-will; (16) some out of love, knowing that I am placed here because of my defense of the Gospel, (17) while others proclaim Christ out of partisanship, not sincerely, thinking that in this way they will add to my trouble in my confinement. (18) What follows? Christ is preached on all sides, sincerely or insincerely, and so I will rejoice.

(19) Yea, I rejoice in this, for I know that 'this will turn out to be my salvation' (Job 13:16) through your prayer

and through the supplying of the Spirit of Jesus Christ. (20) I
hope and I am sure that I shall not be put to shame, but that
with full courage, now as always, Christ will be glorified in
my body, whether I live or die.

(21) For me to live is Christ, and to die is gain.
(22) But if I live in the flesh, this is fruit of labor for me—and
which course I shall take I do not know. (23) I am torn
between two desires: the desire to go and to be with Christ,
which is much better for me, (24) and the desire to stay in
the flesh, which is better for you. (25) Because I am convinced
of this, I expect to stay on with you all, for your progress and
joy in the faith. (26) Thus your pride in me may abound in
Christ Jesus, because of my coming back to you.

(27) Only live worthily of the Gospel of Christ,
regardless of whether I come to see you or must be content
with hearing about you. Stand in the Spirit, being all of one
mind as you fight together for the faith of the Gospel, (28)
and don't be afraid of your enemies in any issue. This will be
a clear sign to them, from God, of their destruction and of your
salvation. (29) For to you is given the privilege not simply of
believing in Christ but of suffering for him, (30) waging the
same conflict which you saw me fight and you hear that I am
now fighting.

CHAPTER II

(1) If then you find any help in Christ, any stimulus of love, any fellowship of the Spirit, any mercy and kindness toward you, (2) make my joy complete by having this same thought and love and mind toward one another. (3) Have just one object: that nothing shall be done out of ill-temper or egotism, and that everything shall be done in true humility, (4) each one of you considering others ahead of himself and seeking their welfare rather than his own.

(5) Have in yourselves this mind which is also in Christ Jesus, (6) who, being in form of God, did not consider it any over-reaching of himself to be equal with God; (7) yet he emptied himself, took the form of a slave, and was born in likeness of men. (8) And being found in appearance as man he humbled himself, becoming subject to death—death by a cross. (9) For this reason God has exalted him pre-eminently, and has honored him with the Name above every name, (10) so that in the Name of Jesus every knee should bow, of creatures in heaven and on earth and under the earth, (11) and every tongue should confess, to the glory of God the Father, that JESUS CHRIST IS LORD.

(12) So then, my beloved, as you were always obedient when I was with you, be even more so in absence and
work out your own salvation with fear and trembling. (13) It
is God working in you who causes you both to want, and to
work for, his approval.

(14) Do everything without grumbling and argu-
ment, (15) so that you may be free from fault, straightforward,
unspoiled children of God living among an unenlightened and
twisted people. (16) Among such you appear as bright stars
in the world, holding out to them the word of life. This will
be my boast in the day of Christ, the proof that I did not run
and work in vain. (17) And if my life is poured out as a libation upon the sacrifice and service of your faith, I am glad,
and I rejoice with you all. (18) For this same reason, be glad
and rejoice with me.

(19) I hope in the Lord Jesus to send Timothy to
you soon, so that I may be cheered by hearing about your
affairs. (20) I have no one else of congenial mind who will
honestly put your welfare first. (21) All the others serve their
own interests rather than the interests of Jesus Christ. (22) But
you know his worth, and how he worked with me as a child
with his father in the service of the Gospel. (23) Therefore
I hope to send him as soon as I see how my own situation
develops; (24) but I trust in the Lord that I will soon be

169

coming to you myself. (25) Even so, I have decided that I must send to you Epaphroditus, my brother and co-worker and fellow soldier, and your messenger and minister to my need. (26) For he has been longing for all of you, and distressed because you heard that he was ill. (27) He was, in fact, sick nearly to death, but God had mercy on him—and on me, so that I should not suffer grief piled upon grief. (28) So I sent him all the sooner, that you may have the pleasure of seeing him again and I may be less anxious. (29) Receive him in the Lord most joyfully, and hold such men in honor, (30) for he came near to death for the word of Christ, risking his life in carrying out your ministry to me in my need.

CHAPTER III

(1) Finally, my brothers, rejoice in the Lord. To write these things to you is not irksome to me, and it is prudent for your sake. (2) Beware of the dogs, beware of the evildoers, beware of the party of the circumcision. (3) For we are the truly circumcised, we who worship God in Spirit and who make our boast, not in a privileged human status, but in Christ Jesus. (4) I happen to have some basis for 'trusting' in that! If anybody else can rely on this, I can make a better claim: (5) circumcised on the eighth day, of the people of Israel, of the tribe of Benjamin, a Hebrew of Hebrews, a Pharisee con-

cerning the Law, (6) a zealous persecutor of the Church, a perfect practitioner of that righteousness of the Law. (7) But whatever I then considered a profit to me, I now consider loss for Christ's sake.

(8) Indeed, I count everything to be worthless compared to the incomparable treasure of knowing Christ Jesus my Lord, for whom I have given up everything. I count it all as refuse in order to gain Christ (9) and to be found in him having, not a righteousness of my own coming from the Law, but that righteousness which comes through faith in Christ—the righteousness given by God and resting on a man's faith. (10) This is the righteousness of knowing him, the power of his resurrection and the fellowship of his sufferings, of being conformed to his dying (11) in such a way that I may possibly attain to the resurrection from the dead.

(12) Not that I have already received the prize, or am already perfect; but I push on that perhaps I might receive it, since I have been received myself by Christ Jesus. (13) Brethren, I do not consider myself as one who has received, but one thing I do: forgetting what lies behind me and stretching forward to the things ahead (14) I push on toward the goal, toward the prize of the upward calling of God in Christ Jesus. (15) For all of us who are mature Christians, then, let this be our principle; and if any of you are of another mind, God

will show this to you. (16) Let us make it our rule to walk by the truth we have already learned.

(17) Be imitators of me, brethren, and study those who live in this way since you have us as an example. (18) For, as I have told you many times before and now with tears tell you again, there are many who live as enemies of the cross of Christ. (19) Their end is destruction; their god is their belly; their glory is in their shame, and their minds are fixed on sordid matters.

(20) For our citizenship is established in heaven, whence we await a Saviour, the Lord Jesus Christ, (21) who shall transform the body of our present low estate into conformity to the body of his glory by the working of his power, which is able to subdue all things to himself.

CHAPTER IV

(1) So then, my brothers, whom I love and long for, my joy and crown, my dearly beloved, stand fast in the Lord in this way.

(2) I entreat Euodia and Syntyche, both, to be of one mind in the Lord. (3) Yea, I beg you, true yoke-fellow,

to help those women who have labored at my side in the work
of the Gospel, along with Clement and my other fellow workers
whose names are in the Book of Life.

(4) Rejoice in the Lord at all times. I say it again,
rejoice! (5) Let your gentleness be apparent to all men. The
Lord is at hand. (6) Worry about nothing, but in every prayer
and supplication make your needs known to God thankfully;
(7) and the peace of God, which is beyond all human conception, shall protect your hearts and thoughts in Christ Jesus.

(8) As for the rest, brethren: whatever things are
true, and worthy of reverence, and just, and pure, and lovely,
and well spoken of, if there is any virtue and any praise-
worthiness in these things fix your minds upon them. (9) The
things you have learned and received, and heard and seen, in
me, do; and the God of peace shall be with you.

(10) I rejoice heartily in the Lord that now you have
revived your concern for me, which undoubtedly you felt
before but you lacked opportunity to act upon it. (11) Not
that I complain about being in want, for I have learned to be
content in any circumstances whatever. (12) I know how to
be in need and I know how to be in plenty. In everything and
in all things I have learned how to eat and how to go hungry,
how to have plenty and how to have little. (13) In him who

strengthens me I can meet anything. (14) None the less, you did well to share my affliction with me. (15) You know that you Philippians, in the early days of the Gospel when I left Macedonia, were the only church that shared with me in giving and receiving, (16) for even when I was in Thessalonika both once and twice you sent what I needed. (17) I do not seek the gift, but I seek the fruit which abounds to your credit. (18) I have all I need, and more; I am full of the good things I have received from you by the hand of Epaphroditus, 'an odor of fragance,' a sacrifice acceptable and pleasing to God. (19) My God will meet all your need, according to his wealth in glory, in Christ Jesus. (20) Unto God and our Father be glory forever and ever. Amen.

(21) Greet every saint in Christ Jesus. The brethren who are with me greet you. (22) All the saints greet you, especially they who are of Caesar's household. (23) The grace of the Lord Jesus Christ be with your spirit.